THE LOST CAUSE OF RHETORIC

The Relation of Rhetoric and Geometry in Aristotle and Lacan

David Metzger

With a Foreword by
Jasper Neel

Southern Illinois University Press
Carbondale and Edwardsville

LIBRARY OF CONGRESS CATALOGING-IN-PUBLICATION DATA

Metzger, David, date.
   The lost cause of rhetoric : the relation of rhetoric and geometry
in Aristotle and Lacan / David Metzger : with a foreword by Jasper
Neel.
      p.   cm.
   Includes bibliographical references and index.
      1. Narration (Rhetoric). 2. Aristotle. Rhetoric. 3. Lacan,
Jacques, 1901–1981. 4. Geometry. I. Title.
   PN212.M48   1995
   808—dc20   93-38231
   ISBN 0-8093-1855-5   CIP

The paper used in this publication meets the minimum requirements of
American National Standard for Information Sciences—Permanence of Paper
for Printed Library Materials, ANSI Z39.48-1984. ∞

CONTENTS

FOREWORD

Anyone who reads this book will already see the humor (indeed the wildly ludicrous impossibility) of any such thing as a "fore" "word." There is nothing "fore" about this "word," which came many months "aft." Early in his book, David Metzger alludes to a painting entitled *Lenin in Warsaw*. I will ask that you remember this "fore" "word" while laughing at that joke, because, just as Lenin could not be in his Moscow bed on the day when he visited Warsaw, I cannot "be fore" anything written in this book. I can, however, delete one letter and "be for" it, and I am. Anyone interested in rhetoric who misses this book will forever lack the lack that this book will engender. And even in these days when rhetoricians (especially those who call themselves rhet/comp people) are in high demand, no one can miss the embrace of lack that any rhetorician must execute.

The nineties have seen an explosion of excellent books in composition studies. Two of the more thoughtful and thought provoking are Susan Jarratt's *Rereading the Sophists* and Lester Faigley's *Fragments of Rationality*. As a way of articulating composition studies, Jarratt turns to the ancient sophists and Faigley to postmodern critical theory. Each book, however, speaks itself through the voice that Aristotle created in the *Rhetoric* and the *Metaphysics*. Both Jarratt and Faigley write in the serene, lucid middle style. Both write clearly. Each has a thesis. Each explains history and its interpretation. Each also suggests, however, that her or his writing is at best a trope and at worst a deception. Behind Jarratt's book stand the wild excess, the verbal display, and the untamed deconstruction of such Sophists as Protagoras and Gorgias. Before Faigley's book stands the whole "French fried" theoretical matrix that puts writing radically in question. Anyone who reads either Faigley or Jarratt must, in my opinion, ask what writing might look like in a sophistical, postmodern world.

This book by David Metzger begins to answer that question, for Metzger consistently writes about what is gone from the page he is writing; he consistently makes the connection that no one expects or even wants; he consistently, in short, is inconsistent—inconsistency being the only appropriate response to the consistency one might demand based on the simplest, most straightforward notions of writing.

Faigley accuses (rightly, in my opinion) composition studies of being populated by a group of modernists well-read in postmodern theory. Metzger's book is going to test Faigley's accusation, for Metzger writes a postmodern rhetoric *in* a postmodern rhetoric. Naturally this does not suggest a jettisoning of tradition; rather, it requires a (in Jarratt's terms) refiguration of tradition.

Not only does Metzger describe writing at its "zero degree," but he also writes toward that degree, not as Barthes wanted to describe it but as the only way one moves thinking from one to two; zero, as it were, is the "route" Metzger takes from one to two. Metzger writes out (of) the silence of knowledge into the polyvocal confusion of play. He offers nothing more than the excessive, teasing, excitement of desire—a desire not to be satiated but always to be desired.

Who, after all, really wants to "know" the relationship between rhetoric and geometry? Who wants to see the (odd) coupling of Aristotle with Lacan? Who can bear a chapter that announces itself as a (standard topical) comparison-contrast essay on Aristotle and Lacan only to conduct itself as a self-confusing counterplay between Descartes and Derrida?

I think Metzger's book will test the field of composition studies because it executes what many of us—in the most classical sort of rhetoric—have called for. No one who reads the book will "learn anything" because the book unwrites any such notion as "learning something." Let me put it this way. Compare sentences from Gorgias' defense of Helen and Derrida's description of Plato with paragraphs from Plato's *Phaedrus* and Aristotle's *Rhetoric*. Gorgias ends his defense of Helen with this sentence, "By this discourse I have freed a woman from evil reputation: I have kept the promise which I made in the beginning; I have essayed to dispose of the injustice of defamation and the folly allegation; I have prayed to compose a lucubration for Helen's adulation and my own delectation" (*Helen* 19). Derrida ends "Plato's Pharmacy" with sentences like these:

> —I hope this one won't get lost. Quick, a duplicate . . . graphite . . . carbon . . . reread this letter . . . burn it. *Il y a la cendre.* And now, to distinguish, between two repetitions . . .
> The night passes. In the morning, knocks are heard at the door. They seem to be coming from outside, this time . . .
> Two knocks . . . four . . .
> —But maybe it's just a residue, a dream, a bit of dream left over, an echo of the night . . . that other theater, those knocks from without . . . (*Dissemination* 171)

Plato, in contrast, in summing up the conditions required for true rhetoric and writing has his Socrates speak as follows:

> The conditions to be fulfilled are these: first, you must know the truth about the subject that you speak or write about: that is to say, you must be able to isolate it in definition, and having so defined it you must next understand how to divide it into kinds, until you reach the limit of division; secondly you must have a corresponding discernment of the nature of the soul, discover the type of speech appropriate to each nature, and order and arrange your discourse accordingly, addressing a variegated soul in a variegated style that ranges over the whole gamut of tones, and a simple soul in a simple style. . . . Such is the clear purport of all our foregoing discussion. (*Phaedrus* 277b–c)

And look at the way Aristotle describes the components of rhetoric. "It was natural," he explains, "that we should first investigate the subject which comes first in the natural order—the facts themselves as a source of persuasion." Having done that, however, the rhetorician must address "the question, how to set out these facts in language" (*Rhetoric* 1403b). While many of us in composition studies have read the sophists and the deconstructionists, none of us (except, perhaps, for Victor Vitanza) has tried to write the sort of text that the Sophists and the postmodern theorists write and imply. None of us, that is, until now. When Metzger writes, he writes like Gorgias and Derrida (well, he writes better than Derrida, but that's another matter). Most of the rest of us write *about* Gorgias and Derrida, but we write *like* Plato at his most earnest and *like* Aristotle all the time.

In addition to reading the sophists and the "trendy modern theorists," Metzger has decided to write like them as well. To someone like me—someone, that is, who remains an undeconstructed logocentrist—Metzger's book seems like both a "logical" and a "necessary" next step. At any rate, I can recommend this book both to those, like me, who seek out and live in the quite traditional, classical world, with all its contradictions; and to those who wonder what living (and writing) in the sophistical, postmodern world might be like.

As I read most recent books in composition studies, I hear the disinterested, knowledgeable, thesis-driven voice that Aristotle created in *Metaphysics*. I have the image of the solitary scholar/professor who "knows." Metzger, in contrast, writes with a devilish gleam in his eye; he makes clear on every page that either he does not "know" anything or that he knows "something else." When I read Metzger, I have two contradictory images in mind. In the first, I see a dervish juggler frantically dancing his own dance while keeping several bowling pins spinning in the air. Nothing (aside from Metzger) ever hits the ground, but something is on the verge of crashing at every moment. In the second image, I see the protagonist in a French farce who remains forever trapped in a scene that includes three hidden characters from mutually exclusive plots plus a fourth revealed character whose story ties all the plots together. The protagonist rushes around the stage trying to keep the plots and any combination of the other four characters separate, which is also how he holds the play together. The result of the double "juggling" (of idea and plot) makes for a quite wonderful book, the cleverest thing I have read on rhetoric since I first read *Phaedrus*.

JASPER NEEL

INTRODUCTION

THE ARGUMENT

The Lost Cause of Rhetoric is not an answer to the question, What is rhetoric? It is an argument for keeping that question alive. It has been too easy for rhetoricians to follow the lead (at least in this century) of their colleagues in literature departments: Accepting that if there is, in fact, something called rhetoric it can be discussed in terms of historical periods, major figures, or major theoretical orientations. The problem I see in such approaches is that they assume knowledge of what rhetoric is—turning rhetorical inquiry into a chasing after possibilities. "I know what rhetoric is," these researchers tell us. "I just don't know what medieval rhetoric, what feminist rhetoric, what phenomenological rhetoric might be." What is more, this dismissal of what rhetoric *is*—for the sake of what it *might be* (sometimes cleverly disguised as a question of what rhetoric *was*)—has a utopian sense about it—a certain dismissal of the here and now—as if at some time in the future people will be able to shuttle through space and colonize the planet "Rhetoricon 5." However, without some recognition of the problematic that "futurism" obviates (the problem of dealing with the here and now), the "future" of rhetorical studies in the United States is to become, like catfish in the Amazon River, only bigger with age, not better.

In the first chapter, I argue that this dismissal of the "here and now" (and consequently the dismissal of rhetoric itself) takes the form of two basic philosophical moves: the onomastic (which dismisses rhetoric because it is not philosophic) and the genealogical (which dismisses rhetoric because it is philosophic). Using Descartes's *cogito* and Derrida's discussion of genre as examples of those two philosophical moves, I then introduce the work of Lacan

and Aristotle as their counterexamples. In other words, I construct
an *experimentum mentis* of sorts: if those who have denied rhetoric
its status as a type of knowledge find it necessary to embrace
geometry as a paradigm for all modes of inquiry, then it may be
possible to observe how rhetoric is constructed as a type of knowledge by examining the work of those people who have thought
rhetoric and geometry to be more similar than dissimilar.

With this experiment in mind, I chose to discuss Aristotle
and Lacan. This is not to say there are not others who could serve
as examples. But Lacan's careful reading of Aristotle, particularly
Lacan's examination of the *Nicomachean Ethics* in his *Seminar
XX*, convinced me to work principally with those two thinkers. In
addition, I thought it prudent to deal with Aristotle whose work
has been firmly placed in most canons of rhetoric, so that I might,
by virtue of comparison, argue that Lacan—who is not commonly
thought of as a rhetorician of any sort—did indeed formulate a
rhetoric. In fact, I would argue that Lacan has greater claim to the
status of rhetorician than many of those whom Bizzell and Herzberg
anthologize in their *Rhetorical Tradition*.

In chapters 2 and 3, I argue that rhetoric is about the present—
how it binds us and cuts into us. For Lacan, rhetoric was a means
of delineating, through the "laws" of metaphor and metonymy, the
instance of the letter, the instant(s) or "nowness" of the unconscious
understood as *zeitlos*, a timeless and tireless worker. For Aristotle,
rhetoric was a *dunamis*, a faculty and potentiality, but not a potentiality with reference to the future. Aristotle's notion of potentiality
is aligned on the side of the now, the body, the infinite, and the
particular, all of which escape the symbolic order of other genres
of inquiry (physics, metaphysics, and logic, for example). In this
manner, the structural properties of rhetoric for both Lacan and
Aristotle appear in rhetoric's relation to geometry. Mathematicians,
after all, know the "instant of the letter" as the derivative of a
function, which has as its counterpart a geometric slope. And it
is precisely as a *dunamis* that Aristotle is able to structure the
contradictory present and presence of geometric lines, which are
infinite in division but not infinite in their extension.

Chapter 4 presents an argument for the scientific status of

rhetoric. The chapter has two controlling propositions: (1) a method of inquiry concerned with attributing truth values to existence claims must do so with reference to some "nothingness," some empty set; (2) rhetoric and geometry are uniquely suited to accept such a challenge.

THE SUBJECT

The subject of *The Lost Cause* is the relation of rhetoric and geometry. But in what sense subject?

There is a painting hanging in a Moscow gallery called *Lenin in Warsaw*. Lenin, it may surprise some people, does not appear in the painting. In the painting, one sees Lenin's wife in bed with some other man.[1] Yet, I would say the subject of this painting is, indeed, "Lenin in Warsaw," since his wife is in Moscow. That is, an object of representation may seem present in its absence: both as a precondition and, one might say, as a lost cause. The subject of the painting, in this sense, is repressed (a metonymy). It is a signifier placed under a bar (the signifier of substitution) allowing another signifier to put its big pants on and become the subject (a metaphor).

As the subject of this book, the relation between rhetoric and geometry operates in much the same way. Those looking for "the twelve similarities between rhetoric and geometry" will be disappointed. The relation of rhetoric and geometry has been in the trash can of philosophy for quite some time. And its place in theoretical discourse appears in terms of the part it has played in the evocation of other subjects: (1) desire/demand; (2) infinities of the ONE/ infinities of the many; (3) possibility/potentiality; (4) contingency/ necessity; (5) god/the unconscious; (6) life/death; (7) imperatives/ interrogatives.

All of these "themes" will be brought up in the first chapter where I will reintroduce into their enumeration an empty set, a big fat zero, which I call "the relation between rhetoric and geometry." This is the essence of my approach to the subject matter: something can function and not exist . . . even something as ludicrous and important as the relation of rhetoric and geometry. I address the function of empty sets and zeros quite specifically in chapters 3 (where I introduce Lacan's formalization of the object a̱) and 4 (where I examine their use in truth-functional logics). But I think I should say a little something here as well.

THE METHOD

I have tried to construct a methodological approach from one of Lacan's statements about identity: "A signifier is a subject for another signifier." When I say that my method is to introduce a zero-function into a series, then I am trying to elaborate a third term in a relation among signifiers. I am rereading Lacan's statement as "where there was one, there are now two." And it seems to me that a person cannot get from one to two without a zero. Later in the text I will seek justification for this notion in the work of Frege, Lacan, Peano, and Kant, among others. For now, just as a means to introduce the point, one might see what I'm talking about in Aristotle's concern about the relation of reference to truth: "For the same statement (logos) seems to be both true and false. Suppose, for example, that the statement that somebody is sitting is true; after he has got up this statement will be false. Similarly with beliefs. Suppose you believe truly that somebody is sitting; after he has got up you will believe falsely if you hold the same belief about him" (4a23–8). Where there was one "(non)sitting" there is now two: "sitting" as statement and "sitting" as action. The zero is represented here as the emerging absence of a reference for the statement "x is now sitting." Again, this is not an unproblematic reading of Aristotle, but I will save my elaboration of the point for chapter 3, where I discuss—among other things—Aristotle's thoughts on the relation of body, motion, and time.

Some Lacanians have called the "method" I propose "reading desire" or "reading topologically." Topology, one might say, is a means of identifying geometric figures according to their number of holes; desire is an endless call to the absent Other ([w]hole). Both have a lot to do with how a person goes from one thing to another, how a person becomes one thing from another.

In this study, I will read looking for deadlocks and impasses in thought, cuts and disjunctures: Why does Aristotle stop with God? Why does Merleau-Ponty stop with possibility? Why does Derrida stop with imperatives? Why does Kant stop with concepts? Why does academic discourse stop with a master signifier? Why does the scientist stop with his or her desire? These stops, these zeros are precisely—I would say—what help us to make our way in the world. They allow us to mark our place in a story that is our symptom (our guarantee of meaning, summation); they allow us to mark our position along a trail we think we are clearing only for ourselves. And they help us to find the way of our desire. This is not, however, to say we all stop at the same place.

In fact, one might look at *The Lost Cause* as my particular elaboration of two stop signs that I've encountered in my own thinking about and teaching of writing: "Writing as Desire" and "Writing as Symptom."

ACKNOWLEDGMENTS

I thank Lynda and Michael Sexson, who even now help me to see there is always one more good book to read. I also thank Ellie Ragland-Sullivan for the precision with which she has addressed the difficulties of Lacan's teaching. And, finally, I thank Alicia, Eliot, R. C., and my parents for their continuing support.

LACANIAN MATHEMES AND OTHER SYMBOLS USED IN THIS STUDY

Lacan's Four Discourse Structures (taken from *Seminar XX*)

Discourse of the Master

$$\frac{S1}{\$} \xrightarrow{\text{impossibility}} \frac{S2}{\underline{a}}$$

Discourse of the Academy

$$\frac{S2}{S1} \xrightarrow{} \frac{a}{\$} \quad \text{impotence}$$

Discourse of the Hysteric

$$\frac{\$}{\underline{a}} \xrightarrow{} \frac{S1}{S2} \quad \text{impotence}$$

Discourse of the Analyst

$$\frac{a}{S2} \xrightarrow{\text{impossibility}} \frac{\$}{S1}$$

The Discourse Positions:

agent	other
truth	production

Additional Mathemes and Symbols

fantasy: $ ◇ a̲
the barred big Other (Autre): A
the barred subject: $
the losange (alienation [\/] and separation [/\]: ◇
the object a̲ (cause of desire, *plus-de-jouir*): a̲
knowledge: S2
master signifier: S1

Words set in capital letters, namely, WOMAN, ONE, RHET-
ORIC, and MAN, mean the essential or completely described concept of something.

THE LOST CAUSE OF

RHETORIC

1

THE LOST CAUSE OF RHETORIC

In the following chapters, I will examine how Lacan and Aristotle have established a relation between rhetoric and geometry in such a way that the geometrical helps to specify what a rhetoric is rather than what it is not. In fact, as we will see in my investigation of Descartes and Derrida in this chapter, the question of rhetoric's relation to geometry makes apparent two very powerful obstacles to the development of rhetoric as a method of inquiry: its conception as either mundane or esoteric.[1] The mundane, after all, does not need to be spoken about, and the esoteric might just as well not have been.

However, it is possible to use such notions as the "mundane" and the "esoteric" for the further examination of rhetoric. If rhetoric is so easily placed along the axes of the esoteric and the mundane, I would like to know why. What does this twin aspect of rhetoric's own rhetorical stance say about rhetoric? At this point, it need not be of concern that I have not defined what I mean by rhetoric because I do not intend to rename rhetoric by saying what *it will be* nor even to rename it by saying what *it was*. Of course, giving rhetoric its first and last names is important. But I am more interested in investigating rhetoric as the effects of the name philosophy has already given it. In fact, I will argue that the apparent ease with which rhetoric is mapped onto the axes of mundaneness and esoter-

1

icism is a result of the philosophization of rhetoric. Furthermore, this philosophization consists of two general moves from which the logical structure of the philosophical is derived: the onomastic and the genealogical.

One of the challenges faced when speaking of some such thing as "a philosophical tradition" is to demonstrate that what might be said of three or four philosophers is somehow indicative of philosophy in general. With this in mind, I've chosen to use the work of Derrida and Descartes as examples of the philosophization of rhetoric. For now, I will be satisfied to suggest that if two philosophers of such different ilks as Derrida and Descartes make the same recourse to geometry with the same reduction of rhetoric to some silent place, then there must be something about philosophy itself as a genre of inquiry that (structurally speaking and thus not accounted for by what some would think to be the content of philosophy) precludes the formalization of rhetoric as a mode of inquiry—that is, makes rhetoric either mundane or esoteric.

The onomastic wishes rhetoric away by establishing the *possibility* for absolute clarity and expression of thought. Rhetoric is not necessary, in those terms, because language itself is capable of persuading and communicating if it is carefully constructed as a set of names (*onoma*) for a corresponding set of things. Rhetoric is a mere frivolity, an unnecessary and often mistaken codification of what is an effect of thought. It is a naming of naming, when one, such as Descartes, comes down to brass tacks. Rhetoric is a rarefied, esoteric object, in these terms.

The genealogical, on the other hand, wishes rhetoric away by establishing the *impossibility* for absolute clarity and expression of thought. Rhetoric is not necessary, in those terms, because language itself is incapable of persuading and communicating even if it is carefully constructed as a set of names for a corresponding set of things. There is no need to think of rhetoric as an obscure object here because it is only a metonymy for the impossibility of communication in general; rhetoric is the mundane object, in these terms. My later discussion of Derrida's work as an example of the genealogical move will be helpful in further specifying its

2

characteristics, particularly since throughout his career Derrida has said that he works within a philosophical tradition.[2]

In this chapter, I will outline the three-part procedures of the onomastic and genealogical moves. In addition, I intend to show how geometry figures prominently in each of the two philosophical moves as an alternative to the rhetorical when, in fact, it is philosophy that is rhetoric's altern, not geometry. Rhetoric, I will observe in Lacan and Aristotle later, can be seen as a questioning of philosophical examinations of relationality, which lead, in turn, to a rhetorical formation of causality (as choice and time). This is not to say that relations are always known to philosophy or that philosophy cannot ask questions about relationality. However, in philosophical discourse, relationality takes the place of the known and causality takes the place of the unknown. That is, philosophy constructs problems by situating the object of its inquiry in a causal position within a particular context and then solves them by redescribing the object of its inquiry (cause) as a particular relationality within another context.

Another aspect of philosophical discourse that will become apparent in my investigation of Descartes and Derrida is its privileging of one kind of infinity over another. In Descartes, an infinity of the one, of metaphor, the infinity of laws and the possibility of their infinite application accompanies his dismissal of rhetoric. Likewise, in Derrida, an infinity of the many, of metonymy, the infinity of laws as their own (dis)placed applications replaces what I will later call an "infinity of the numerous and of the particular," an infinity that then keeps company with rhetoric in the trash can of philosophy.

I will now describe this maneuvering of causality, relationality, and infinity more specifically in terms of the onomastic and genealogical moves and demonstrate how philosophy's treatment of cause and relation effects the dismissal of rhetoric as either esoteric or mundane.

DESCARTES AND THE ONOMASTIC MOVE

> a sketch of the onomastic: cause/effect; metaphor/meton-
> ymy; rhetoric as esoteric; infinity

The onomastic move addresses the question, "Who Dunnit?"
a question that immediately puts us within that murder mystery,
philosophy, as Sophocles represented it so powerfully in his *Oedipus Rex*. "Who Dunnit's," unfortunately, are based on an error in
categorization—a confusion of the causal, which is assumed to be
unknown, and the relational, which is assumed to be known. Simply
because of a particular contiguous relation with the murder victim
(which would render an individual in relation to an event), an
individual is treated as a cause and a metaphor (a suspect). The
dimension of effect here is written as an act of predication. Effect
is a list of adjectives representing the various possibilities of The
Metaphoric One—being or substance.[3] This is not to say onomastic
philosophies commit the fallacy of *post-hoc-ergo-propter hoc*. On
the contrary, I would say the onomastic move treats effects as if
they were *logically* prior to their causes and predicates as if they
were *logically* prior to that which they predicate; in other words, not
only is the onomastic primarily metaphoric, but it is also primarily
deductive.[4]

Unfortunately, this logical program can never provide a formalization of rhetoric because it hides our need for rhetoric in the
acme of clarity, the transparent relation of one thing being as
another: rhetoric is Y; time is Z; philosophy is B; and my love is
a red, red rose.[5] In those terms, rhetoric is said not to be a science
because its cause(s) cannot be rendered as metaphors concealed as
definitions or laws.[6] This is not to say people can't define rhetoric
and specify its laws (people do it every day), but such would be
a philosophical act and important in terms of some larger philosophical project, as we will see.

Metaphors, after all, must be grounded on some exception
that proves their rule.[7] More particularly, in terms of onomastic
philosophies, something has to be thrown out as a non-cause so

that a cause might be established. And rhetoric is precisely that some/thing getting thrown out. I do not mean that to know some/thing (philosophy) one must know its opposite (rhetoric), though at times Plato seems only to be saying as much. What I am talking about is more in the manner of certain set theories where to recognize even the function of the null set in a counting system, there must be an a-prime (a) to precede it; nothing is not the same thing as nothingness.[8] Onomastic philosophy, in this light, is the use of rhetoric to try to speak the cause of philosophy lost to its own logic (a cause displaced by the a priori status of effect and predicate)— that cause of philosophy, rhetoric.

Of course, rhetoric cannot be left for long in this place of philosophy's lost cause else it should become philosophy and no longer useful, as a non-cause, for further philosophization. Rhetoric itself must be turned into a question (a non-cause, if you will), which is done easily enough: What, then, is rhetoric's cause? But isn't such a question also an invitation to some sort of infinite regress? Indeed, might the notion of a rhetorical question—which itself is not to be answered—be simply one way to avoid such a regress? By putting rhetoric in its place, the infinite, isn't philosophy then off the hook? Leaving rhetoricians with only a busy signal? Having addressed that question, I will then have specified the onomastic move and its treatment of rhetoric both in terms of its content and its methodology. I will use Descartes's *cogito* and his famous solution to the "Pappus-locus" problem as examples of the onomastic move and its particular use of knowable relations to discover unknown causes, since there can be no question that these two Cartesian projects are securely placed in the philosophical tradition.

DESCARTES AS AN EXAMPLE OF THE ONOMASTIC: HIS *COGITO*

Earlier, I suggested that the onomastic move has as one of its results the mundaneness of rhetoric. We will see the mechanism for such a conception of rhetoric in the *cogito* argument Descartes presents in his *Meditations*:

5

(1) It is true that no one can be certain that he is thinking or that he exists unless he knows what thought is and what existence is. But this does not require reflective knowledge, or the kind of knowledge that is acquired by means of demonstrations; still less does it require knowledge of reflective knowledge, i.e. knowing that we know, and knowing that we know that we know, and so on *ad infinitum*. This kind of knowledge cannot possibly be obtained about anything.

(2) It is quite sufficient that we should know it by that internal awareness which always precedes reflective knowledge. This inner awareness of one's thought and existence is so innate in all men that, although we may pretend that we do not have it if we are overwhelmed by preconceived opinions and pay more attention to words than to their meanings, we cannot in fact fail to have it.

(3) Thus when anyone notices that he is thinking and that it follows from this that he exists, even though he may never before have asked what thought is or what existence is, he still cannot fail to have sufficient knowledge of them both to satisfy himself in this regard. (69)

For the purposes of this discussion it is not important to determine if Descartes's argument is really an argument. It is sufficient, for us, to determine that Descartes's assumption of proof is a specification of causality in terms of relationality, using our supposed knowledge of the latter to offset our ignorance of the former. That is, after imagining the unknowable cause, "therefore," was knowable as a relation between "I think" and "I am," Descartes easily establishes the *cogito* as a knowable relation between itself and its unknowable cause that is, in turn, made knowable as a relation between itself as thinking and itself as being. I may seem to imply that the *cogito* is some elaborate bait and switch. I hope to demonstrate that the *cogito* is more an illustration of how metonymies can put on the clothing of a metaphor—as the three parts of the *cogito* will make apparent in terms of their manipulation of causality and relationality:

1. Introduction of the problem: Thinking as a Knowable Relation with Thinking. If I conceive of thinking as thinking of something, where or when can I stop thinking of thinking of thinking

of . . . ? Such knowledge would not put us in a place from which to be in order to think such a thing.

2. Development of the problem: Thinking may be known in terms of a knowledge that precedes reflective thought. A person just has to think about what kind of knowledge might precede reflective thought. The cause is here established as the object of the philosopher's inquiry. That is, if Descartes could only find out what causes reflective thought, then he would know in what sense "I think; therefore, I am" is as true as he suspects it is.

3. Resolution of the problem: Having dispensed with relationality as something absolutely knowable as itself but not as knowledge, Descartes posits a before (or a cause) to relationality, which he called in (2) an "inner awareness." But, curiously enough, to make this inner awareness into something he might, in turn, have knowledge of, Descartes must render it as a relation that, with regard to Allan Bloom, might be called a person's "ontological literacy": anyone who can think the *cogito* has sufficient knowledge to understand what it means. But where is the cause in such an assertion? In (2), Descartes writes that he was going to find what preceded reflective thought. He discovers innate thought, which he easily translates into a predicate of thinking. Thus, what Descartes wanted to know as a cause in (2) is somehow known when it is expressed as a predicate relation in (3)—a metonymy (predicate) treated as a substitution metaphor (cause).

Furthermore, the name for this curious logical maneuvering is the *cogito*, hence the self-evident quality of the assertion. The second name for this knowable relational cause is "God." In that form, God can serve as the system within which such an imagining has a certain evidentiary force insofar as the causal is established as a function of the relational. "Who Dunnit?" one might ask. Replies Descartes, "God, you silly goose":

> Moreover, in inquiring about what caused me I was not simply asking about myself as a thinking thing; principally and most importantly I was asking about myself in so far as I observe, amongst my other thoughts, that there is within me the idea of a supremely perfect being. The whole force of my proof depends on this one fact. For, firstly, this idea contains the essence of

7

> God, at least in so far as I am capable of understanding it; and
> according to the laws of true logic, we must never ask about
> the existence of anything until we first understand its essence.
> Secondly, it is this idea which provides me with the opportunity
> of inquiring whether I derive my existence from myself, or from
> another, and of recognizing my defects. And lastly, it is this
> same idea which shows me not just that I have a cause, but that
> this cause contains every perfection, and hence that it is God.
> (*Meditations* 88)

Descartes is particularly clever here. He takes the rather commonplace notion of God's omnipresence and constructs a theory
of demonstration from it. Descartes's God is the set of the relations
between relationality and causality. Or, if I might approach the
nonsensical here, "God becomes relationality itself," for Descartes.[9] And The Golden Rule, in his hands, becomes an onto-
epistemology, which is the goal of any onomastic move—to speak
clearly, without the intervention of rhetoric or the need for rhetoric:
"I esteemed Eloquence most highly and I was enamored of Poesy,
but I thought that both were gifts of the mind rather than fruits of
study. Those who have the strongest power of reasoning, and who
most skillfully arrange their thoughts in order to render them clear
and intelligible, have the best power of persuasion even if they can
but speak the language of Lower Brittany and have never learned
Rhetoric" (*Discourse on Method* 43).

DESCARTES AS AN EXAMPLE OF THE ONOMASTIC:
THE PAPPUS-LOCUS PROBLEM

There is a similar constitution of causality and relationality
in Descartes's solution to the Pappus-locus problem.[10] I would like
to introduce Descartes's work on geometry at this point so that the
similarities between it and his *cogito* might be underscored and
rhetoric might be found, not under the walnut shell of geometry
but between a philosopher's sheets. David Lachterman describes
the challenge of the Pappus-locus problem as follows:

> What challenged Descartes most deeply were two remarks by
> Pappus, first that when more than four lines are given in the

problem the resulting loci "are not known up to the present time but are merely called 'lines' (*grammai*) or linear loci" (Descartes calls them "supersolid loci"). And second, when more than six lines are given, the figures contained by these—not being either plane figures or solids—are incomprehensible, since they would be of more than three dimensions. (Pappus then adds, prophetically, that these higher-order problems can be handled by means of "compounding" ratios.) (Lachterman 146)

Descartes's particular contribution to the Pappus-locus problem demonstrates his contribution to the geometrical method in general, as well as his particular debt to the onomastic. For his renaming of loci in terms of a relation between lines, circles, ellipses, and other geometric figures allows him to map unknowns in terms of a relationality taken for granted in the proportions specified by his "equations":

> The rest of this story is generally familiar. Descartes shows us how to write "equations" for each of the unknown lines so that its length can be determined by the "roots" of these equations. Even more remarkable, Descartes discovers a strict correlation between the number of lines involved in the problem, the degree of the equation of the curve on which the points lie (where the degree of an equation is determined by the highest exponent that occurs in it), and the degree of the simplest curve that can be used in actually constructing the locus defined by the corresponding equation. (Lachterman 147)

Thus, Descartes's genius for perceiving relations and his assumption that the relational is always in a place of the known leads him to make the rather bold statement about his solution to the Pappus-locus problem: "It is only necessary to follow the same course in order to construct all problems, more and more complex, *ad infinitum*" (*Oeuvres*, vol. 6, p. 485). Descartes, I suppose, is here talking about a different sort of infinity than he had dismissed in the first part of his *cogito*. For the sake of making a distinction, one might say that the infinity Descartes dismisses in the first part of his *cogito* ("knowing that we know, and knowing that we know that we know, and so on *ad infinitum*. This kind of knowledge cannot possibly be obtained about anything.") is an infinity of the numerous whereas what he extols as the greatest advantage of his geometric method is an infinity of the one—an infinite application leading us to a singular and essential "applicand," if there is such a word. What is more, this distinction is borne out in Descartes's own description of rhetoric and poesy, albeit obliquely, which says both are "gifts of the mind rather than fruits of study." As a "gift of the mind," rhetoric would be "numbered" as an infinity rather than an infinite, yet well-defined, set of things circumscribed by the activity of study.[11] And, as a "gift," rhetoric seems more frivolous, more *esoteric* window dressing than a legitimate academic pursuit—concerned with a knowledge, a type of infinity, that cannot possibly be attained about anything.

Indeed, this diversion from infinite particularity is marked by the entrance of mathematics into the Cartesian system, as I had suspected earlier in my discussion of how rhetorical questions might be used to obturate a specific kind of infinity. One might say that the infinity proscribed by a well-defined set is knowable as a particular and knowable relation between the genus and species of its definition, and the other kind of infinity is not a relation in the place of the known and is not, therefore, knowable in terms of a philosophical discourse. It is an infinity that marks the entrance of rhetoric into language study, at least insofar as both rhetoric and that particular kind of infinity come out of the same philosophical trash can.

DERRIDA AND THE GENEALOGICAL MOVE

a sketch of the genealogical: infinity; causality; relationality; chance

---

The genealogical move, just like its philosophical counterpart—the onomastic, makes causes knowable by treating them as relations. And it substitutes the infinity (of the particular) for the infinity (of the set), again just as we have already observed in the onomastic. For this reason, the claims of the genealogical are no less extravagant although, perhaps, more familiar to us than the onomastic. We are often required to spend a great deal of our time recording what others think. We are, in this manner, encouraged to append our thinking, in the form of a codicil, to the will/Will of philosophy—leaving all philosophy's belongings to rhetoric if rhetoric were to die. This description of rhetoric as a philosophical accretion is not unlike that acquisition of signifiers some would call "learning." For this reason, the genealogical move has served many people rather well.

However, another aspect of this philosophical move is not so helpful. Exemplified best by Derrida's notion of "grafting," the genealogical attempts to close off interpretation by placing every utterance in quotation marks so that *words*, sequestered from the abuses of desire yet metonymized as desire, might be spoken in and of themselves.[12] This is all to say, "'Heads' and philosophy wins; 'Tails' rhetoric loses." A most curious logic! But it is, I believe, the form a logic must take when the question of rhetoric and geometry becomes (indeed, any rhetorical question becomes) simply a question not to be answered (mundane: something everybody knows; esoteric: something only very few people can understand). Let me explain.

I used a coin toss to denote the logic of this genealogical move toward philosophization because a coin toss not only demonstrates the binary aspect of such a logic but its dissolution of the "accidental" as well (not "the assumption of," which would constitute "rigor," theoretically speaking) in "systematic" philosophical inquiry. Such philosophical dissolutions of accident are all around us. For example, in the United States, it is quite common to hear people talking about "having a fifty-fifty chance"; that is, by virtue of their "having" chance, people curiously take possession of something that by definition is beyond their ken. Having a chance also designates a particular relationship between being and having that structures contingency as a finitude of signifiers: a 13,456,924-to-1 chance, after all, is still countable as such. That is why the phrase "It is not by accident" is as common in *Of Grammatology* as the neologism *différance*. What would be at stake for those people if they were to say with equal confidence that chance, in some ways, has us all—that chance (really more in the

11

sense of a chance/traumatic encounter, here) is, in some fashion, a cause, something that can effect change? What might we lose if causality, as such, is not uncertain but our relation to it is? What might we gain? Rhetoric, I would say.[13]

WHY IS THE GENEALOGICAL ANTI-RHETORICAL? RHETORIC AS MUNDANE

I would argue that rhetoric emerges or is formed by the question of relationality. I will go into this further when I, as a rhetorician, read Lacan in chapter 3. But, for now, let it suffice to say that we can begin to suspect rhetoric is a questioning of relationality qua relation (and not simply relationality as a knowable projection of some unknown cause) because we can observe a great deal of rhetoric (or better said, "a great deal of what constitutes the position of rhetoric") when the relations specified in a genealogy are put into question: "Who should succeed whom as a successor to the throne?" "Who should be the next president?" "Who should be the next Pope?" "Who, Mr. Tisias, should succeed in possession of the back forty since it was acquired during the reign of a tyrant who has just been overthrown?"

Rhetoric, in other words, is established when our social links are "knotted" into the form of a question: "Am I alive or dead?" "Am I a Man or a Woman?" These are the sorts of questions that I would term "rhetorical," questions that must be answered in spirit and bone, in body and action.[14] For this reason, rhetoric must be treated as a given (a lost cause, an exception that proves the rule, an itch to be scratched) if philosophy is to have a reason for being. This is not to say simply, as do some of Derrida's less ambitious exegetes, that "philosophy denies it is in some way literary"—though such, in part, is an effect of what I've said here. To say that everything is rhetoric or to say that rhetoric is the cause of everything is simply another way to wish rhetoric would disappear, insofar as such an assertion is easily translated into "everyone is a rhetorician, so how can we offer Ph.D.'s in it; rhetoric by its nature is not a specialized field of study." I don't mean to indicate that the dismissal of rhetoric as mundane is the necessary conclusion drawn from the assertion, "rhetoric is the cause of everything." Arguments for the interdisciplinary status of rhetorical studies are often rationalized by a similar admission.[15] But notice how such a logic *can* lead one to be silent about rhetoric on account of the subject's mundaneness. If everyone is a rhetorician, if everything is rhetorical, then why bother telling someone something they already know?[16]

No, I'm not saying simply that philosophy defies its rhetoricity. Philosophy denies that it is philosophical; it defies us to make evident the genealogical (and the onomastic) structure of its method and object of inquiry. Isn't such an examination, in part, what deconstruction has shown? At least, Derrida has said as much. We must not assume, however, that a discourse's making apparent the genealogical move is not itself a product of its philosophization. In fact, I can use Derrida's essays "The White Mythology" and "The Law of Genre" as examples of the genealogical move in philosophical discourse. The first essay establishes without question that the object of deconstructive inquiry is an unknown cause. The second essay provides us with a more specific rendering of the philosophical movement of deconstruction in terms of a three-part argument/methodology correlative to the three-part structure of the *cogito* wherein one type of infinity is substituted for another and geometry replaces rhetoric as a method for scientific (knowledge-making) inquiry.

DERRIDA AS AN EXAMPLE OF THE GENEALOGICAL

Indeed, as Derrida himself describes it, the object of his work in "The White Mythology" is an unknown cause or origin: a "tropic and prephilosophical resource [which] could not have the archeological simplicity of a proper origin, the virginity of a history of beginnings" (*Margins of Philosophy* 229). What is more, as did Descartes, Derrida transforms this object of his inquiry into a methodological problem whose solution is to be found in our understanding of relations, asking, "how are we to decipher figures of speech, and singularly metaphor, in the philosophic text?" given that "the exergue [is] effaced" (*Margins of Philosophy* 219). For this reason,

13

it is not in the formalization of a rhetoric that Derrida believes he will find an answer: "Neither a rhetoric of philosophy nor a metaphilosophy appear pertinent here—such is the hypothesis. In the first place, why not rhetoric as such? Each time that a rhetoric defines metaphor, not only is a philosophy implied, but also a conceptual network in which philosophy itself has been constituted" (*Margins of Philosophy* 230).

The genealogical move, as it appears here, is slightly different from the onomastic one—whereas Descartes would fault rhetoric because it is not philosophy, Derrida in his correlative, genealogical move faults rhetoric because it necessarily implies a philosophy. Derrida, then, believes we must look elsewhere than in rhetoric for this tropic source. But where? In his essay "The Law of Genre," he provides us with the methodology for such an investigation, borrowing heavily from catastrophe theory and set theory. Mathematics, it seems, has again come to a philosopher's rescue—at least in the form of an imaginary prosthetic.

For this reason, I will limit my discussion of Derrida's "The Law of Genre" to culling out the "graftings" of catastrophe theory and of set theory with which Derrida creates an intention statement of sorts:

> Before going about putting a certain example to the test, I shall attempt to formulate, in a manner as *elliptical*, economical, and formal as possible, what I shall call the law of the law of genre. It is precisely a principle of contamination, a law of impurity, a parasitical economy. In the code of *set theories*, if I may use it at least figuratively, I would speak of a sort of participation without belonging—a taking part in without being part of, without having membership in a set. The trait that marks membership inevitably divides, the boundary of the set comes to form by *invagination*, an internal pocket larger than the whole; and the outcome of this division and of this abounding remains as singular as it is limitless. (206, emphases mine)

Elliptical. Here, Derrida opens up the same question Descartes did in the first part of his *cogito*: What are the limits of reflective knowledge? If Derrida is interested in the law of the law of genre, why isn't he interested in, as well, the law of the law of the law of the law of. . . ? And what is it about a formal and elliptical "manner" that could obviate the infinite regress he defines? As a means to an answer, let's examine what "elliptical" might mean in this context—particularly, if there is an attempt to imagine "elliptical" as a spatial condition or economy of expression.[17] For one thing, an ellipse might be said to be "a plane curve such that the sums of the distances of each point in its periphery from two . . ." Yes, and then someone might try to draw a picture of it.

A mathematics dictionary might provide another interesting description: "a conic section formed by the intersection of a right circular cone by a plane that cuts obliquely the axis and the opposite sides of the cone" (Daintith and Nelson). There might also be an equation.

The first definition provided is a simple description answering the question, What does an ellipse look like? The second definition is in the form of a picture but a picture still caught in the flypaper of the page. Definition three, while still having the characteristic of a description, also has a noticeable how-to quality not found in the others: "An ellipse is a conic section formed" tells us what tools we need to do the job and how to do it. Definition three is, in essence, an embedded imperative of how to wrench the ellipse from the two-dimensional page and put it into at least three dimensions, at least in terms of who might construct it and with what she might construct it. There is, also, another ellipse. An ellipse that has not been made present so far, and I mean "made present" because this fourth ellipse exists only when we begin to classify those things that we think to be elliptical. Borrowing heavily from Plato, we might observe that the comparison of two or more ellipses would involve the creation (though Plato would call it the recognition) of yet another ellipse that would serve as the classifying principle for those things appearing elliptical. In other words, there must be an ellipse that, because of the nature of the classification process, does not belong to the set of ellipses but that participates in the set of all ellipses. Of course, when it is assumed that an ellipse represents itself and not something else, the ellipse sustaining such curious qualities is the ellipse that functions as the classifying principle of all other ellipses. And in this paradox, Derrida believes he can find a ground from which to form the law of the law of genre.

Set theories. Since Russell used the aforementioned properties of classification to create a formidable paradox in set theory, it is no surprise that Derrida will use Russell's paradox as a model for his discussion of the relation of a work's genre to that work, later transforming Russell's verbal model into his own two-dimensional construct of a catastrophic dynamic of genre—invagination.

Russell, in sum, imagines there are two kinds of classes: classes that do not contain themselves and classes that do. If, and only if, the class does not contain itself as a member, we can call that class "normal." Otherwise, the class will be considered to be "non-normal," indicating that the class is a category that is a part of itself. An example of a "normal class" would be the class of "people who are reading this essay." Obviously, the class itself is not a "person . . . ," so it is a normal class. On the other hand, the class of "all things that can be thought of" would be "non-normal" because the class of "all things that can be thought of" is itself "a thing that can be thought of." Russell then imagines the properties of the set of all normal classes. If someone, for the sake of imagining, were to think that the set of all normal classes is itself a normal class, then that person would need to include the "set of all normal classes" as a member of itself, thereby making the "set of all normal classes" a "non-normal" set. Interestingly, the conclusion is that the "set of all normal classes" is itself normal when it is non-normal and it is non-normal when it is normal. The relation of the class to its member is not one of belonging but one of participation, or as Derrida says of the law of the law of genre, it is "a taking a part in without being part of, without having membership in a set."

In the second scene of his *cogito,* Descartes found "innate knowledge" and thereby directed his attention to the cause of reflective knowledge. Structurally speaking, Derrida's definition of the law of the law of genre is no different from Descartes's "innate knowledge." Derrida even writes that this "law" is a "taking a part" rather than "being a part." What is this but the establishment of an as yet unnamed *pater familias* for genre—a father who has a "great part" to play in reproducing and raising "his children" but who is not a part of them (as the mother is) and must, therefore, legislate his "partness" in the orders of law and incest? But unlike Descartes, Derrida will not call his law of the law, "God." Derrida's god is a trope—chiasmus.

Invagination. The "grammatologist" Greg Ulmer, and others, would have it that Derrida makes "the bold move," in his discussion of invagination, to map Russell's paradox onto a multidimensional model insofar as Derrida writes that the "trait that marks membership inevitably divides, the boundary of the set comes to form, by invagination."[18] Because Derrida chooses to call this process by which a law becomes a form "invagination," Ulmer sees Derrida struggling with the limits of the page at this point—in much the same way as the "embedded imperative" of the third definition of ellipsis did above. The images he presents are clearly multidimensional constructs. It is, after all, difficult even to imagine an "internal pocket larger than the whole," which is two-dimensional. Biologists, however, have tried to present "invagination," as such: for them, invagination is the term for the movement of a blastula to a late gastula, in two dimensions. For this reason, Derrida's proponents have argued that his interest in invagination pushes us from the security of the page to the "bewildering wilds" of a multidimensional model (a model that can account for the creation of a body).[19]

Yet, for all his heroic struggle, doesn't Derrida eventually only come to save the page? Derrida has written that the model of genre produced by invagination is the chiasmus, and it is only when mapped onto a page that a multidimensional model of invagination appears as a chiasmus; such is the graphic lesson catastrophe theorists teach (Thom, *Mathematical Models of Morphogenesis* 139–62).

Here, Derrida presents the chiasmus, which marks a particular topical relation in rhetoric, also a biological origin by virtue of its resemblance to the topological construction of cell's invagination. The uncertainty of an origin is reified as a knowable relation between his philosophical text and Thom's topological/biological one, just as the chiasmus of rhetoric and the chiasmus of philosophy can be identified (made knowable, at least for a moment) in the writing of their supplementary (est, et) relation—what is now a double invagination:

> Each story is part of the other, makes the other a part (of itself), each "story" is at once larger and smaller than itself, includes itself without including (or comprehending itself), identifies itself with itself even as it remains utterly different from its homonym. Of course, at intervals ranging from two to forty paragraphs, this structure of crisscross double invagination . . . never ceases to over-employ itself in the meantime, and the description of this would be interminable. I must content myself for the moment with underscoring the supplementary aspect of this structure: the chiasma of this double invagination is always possible, because of what I have called elsewhere the iterability of the mark. ("The Law of Genre" 217)

If Derrida, then, participates in a philosophical rather than a rhetorical tradition, what can be said of the current interest of rhetoricians in deconstruction? Certainly, deconstruction, the work of Derrida and de Man most particularly, has encouraged the proliferation of "rhetoric" as a term in an exegetical lexicon. However, I believe one should remember that deconstruction has done *just* that. Rhetoric may again be part of a particular theoretical model, but this is not to say the theory itself is rhetorical nor that those who propose to develop and test such a theoretical model are rhetoricians. In fact, it is possible that those who are now talking the most about rhetoric may not be rhetoricians at all, if what they say about rhetoric puts it in the place of a lost cause about which it is impossible to speak (thereby making it possible to speak about philosophy).[20]

Thus, one approaches the importance of writing about the relation of rhetoric and geometry: such a discussion touches on the question of the place of rhetoric and its relation to philosophy. Perhaps, such a question escapes the logic of the Whodunit by virtue of being itself a question and not a constative statement whose veracity is specified simply in terms of the presence or absence of identifiable ontological counterparts for linguistic "presences," imagined and/or symbolic. One might say the veracity (if we can call "it" that) of a question is situated in the real; questions cannot be totalized (except as a symptom), even though their answers may have the appearance of closure. For that reason, we can speak of a question as a performance (a *functio*); it forces us to recognize what it does and what it says by doing. But just as the genealogical has the onomastic as its partner, so the interrogative has a corollary in the imperative. Asking someone a question is easily translated into a command: "Do you think it's hot in here?" might just as well be "Turn the air conditioner on."

What is more, the "multidimensionality" of a text comes in only when one considers the relation of questions and commands. For this reason, I would say, Derrida's notion of a double invagination ("Be fruitful and multiply; draw an ellipse") does not escape the confines of the page; it only considers the imperative dimension of language. It is true that some of us can know, just from the picture on the box, how a chocolate cake we're "whipping up" will turn out. But can we ever know exactly how our demands will be answered/reified by an/other? Even though the investigation may take us off track for awhile, I would like to examine demands and questions for just a bit, since the relation of the two is one of the major structuring devices for chapters 2 and 3.

CONCERNING QUESTIONS AND COMMANDS

Greg Ulmer's "Handbook for a Theory Hobby" demonstrates quite nicely the limitations of studying language only at the level of demand. His "Handbook" is composed mostly of imperatives: "STEP ONE: Make a leaf rubbing." "STEP TWO: Write the word 'leaf' over the rubbing" (406). "STEP THREE: Look up the word 'feal' in an unabridged dictionary" (407). "STEP EIGHT: Reflect on crab grass as a model of a new logic" (415). And so on. Up to STEP TEN. Only at STEP TEN does Ulmer decide his readers "are ready to design some ACTION of [their] own, featuring trees, rubbings, and other related items, practices and information, addressing the problem of writing without paper" (422). The "Handbook" then ends with one final command: "Document the process and file the materials for later use in the theory you are making" (422).

But how does Ulmer decide *when* enough is enough—even though he apparently has some idea of *what* is enough? His list of imperatives could easily have continued on interminably but, like Scheherazade's story telling, it doesn't. I would argue Ulmer's words (his commands) remain glued to the page because they only evoke (what at this point I will call) "bodies" in the name of an action (a motion?) that Ulmer terms, throughout the essay, "writing without paper." Another way to express the point is to say that "Non-writing" does not exist within Ulmer's "the(h)orizin'." Everything is writing. In this manner, Ulmer's tasks may move us away from a certain binarism exemplified by the opposition of writing to non-writing. But the problem of infinite regression looms large in his text (the problem Descartes was able to avoid by making "rhetoric" a "mere ornament to thought"): When does one command not lead into another?

Addressing the relation of questions and time, Derrida's study of the question in Heidegger's work seems to be a response to this difficulty. Yet, Derrida's investigation of the interrogative, without specifying its relation to the imperative, may have its own difficulties, as well.

In his study, *Of Spirit: Heidegger and the Question*, Derrida attributes the otherness of Being to the ex-centric status (the We-ness) of the human subject exemplified by the possibility of a question:

> Now who are we? Here, let us not forget, we are first and only determined from the opening to the question of Being. Even if Being must be given to us for that to be the case, we are only at this point, and know of "us" only this: the power or rather the possibility of questioning, the experience of questioning. (17)

> We were speaking a moment ago of the question. Now precisely this entity which we are, this "we" which, at the beginning of the existential analytic, must have no name other than Da-sein,

is chosen for the position of exemplary entity only from the experience of the question, the possibility of the *Fragen*, as it is inscribed in the network of *Geragte* (being), the *Erfragte* (the meaning of Being), of the *Befragte der Seinsfrage*. (17)

[The Truth of the Truth] belongs to *the beyond* and to the possibility of any question, to the unquestionable itself in any question. (9, emphasis mine)

I underscore Derrida's use of "the beyond" to indicate that again his solution to the philosophical dilemmas represented by infinity (and rhetoric?) is not so much different from Descartes's, perhaps in this instance even more like Descartes than in his discussion of "invagination." "The Beyond," for Derrida, is a metaphor, a treatment of infinity as an identificatory limit: one, two, three, four . . . infinity—grinding on and ground out on the axis of substitution.

Yet, curiously, Derrida does not seem to allow for an infinity-one, infinity-two, infinity-three. Infinity is one (We); it is *the* beyond because to speak of "the beyond" is speaking "the beyond," not *a* speaking *of* the beyond. The beyond, then, does not return to the symbolic, for Derrida. It never left. The beyond isn't itself, except as a name—reinscribing, here, Russell's paradox in set theory, just as Derrida's reliance on the law/demand of genre did.

At one level, *The Lost Cause* is a response to a particular philosophical examination of questions and imperatives. And I have structured the chapters of the book accordingly. My argument is that the relation of questions and commands is seen more at the level of desire than at the level of demand and requires something other than a reading of metaphors and metonymies, nouns and sentences. The relation of questions and commands requires a reading of desire (what appears as a lack in the orders of the symbolic, imaginary, and real) constituting what I would call a "rhetorical reading of philosophy," a study of the choices and substitutions made within the onomastic and genealogical moves of philosophical discourse. The particular configuration of desire and the formation of truth within questions and commands will be explored more critically in chapters 2 and 3.

RHETORIC WITH GEOMETRY

Thus, when I write of "Lacan and the Question of Rhetoric" and "Aristotle's Imperative for Rhetoric," I would propose that a conflict between rhetoric and geometry might be expressed as something other than an answer, as something other than a historical narrative of the philosophical. In fact, "conflict" may not be the only way to name the relation of the two. A person might say, for instance, that the relation of rhetoric and geometry, at least here at the outset, presents us with a rhetorical problem—most definitely a rhetorical question: Why talk about the relation of rhetoric and geometry at all? One reason to study this relation is that the answer to this question seems to establish a place from which to speak about rhetoric—a place that is neither mundane nor esoteric and perhaps both. With this in mind, one can take the argument for rhetoric's mundaneness (everyone must have a place from which to speak) and the argument for its esotericism (rhetoric tries to formalize, in special uses of language, that which cannot be formalized) to present the following proposition: Insofar as geometry is a particular formalization of space and of the relationship of spaces to each other, it would have the potential to provide a formalization of the space(s) of discourse as well and, as a result, a way to talk about the awesome mundaneness of rhetoric. The place of rhetoric would then, in turn, be hollowed out, as an effect of this discourse concerning rhetoric's space.

However, this is not to geometricize rhetoric nor to rhetoricize geometry. I will argue that rhetoric is, in a very particular way, *with* geometry, that is, in the same place as geometry: the place of the residual, the place of those things that drop out of the symbolic order, the place of the real.[21] But from that place, geometry and rhetoric point in opposite directions at the same thing—the void. Geometry and rhetoric are, in this sense, like a glove that when turned inside out is the "same" glove only its "fingers" are pointing in the opposite direction at the same thing—the "that which" surrounds the glove. To specify from what place this "withness" of rhetoric and geometry might be observed is precisely my aim. And, as the metaphor of the glove might have suggested, my methodology will be structural, in as much as "withness," in English at any rate, manifests the structural relations (I might say the structurally syntactic relations, even) of accompaniment and instrumentality.

In chapter 2, "Aristotle's Imperative for Rhetoric," I will establish the conditions for Aristotle's particular difficulty in defining rhetoric as a thing that does, in fact, exist within his system. This will include an examination of Aristotle's use of the term *dunamis* in his *Metaphysics*, since a *dunamis* is precisely what Aristotle says rhetoric is. What is more, Aristotle's use of an imperative ("Let rhetoric be a *dunamis*," Aristotle writes, rather than the declarative, "rhetoric is a *dunamis*") commonly used in geometry texts of his time as the syntactic form of his famous definition of rhetoric can be explained in terms of Aristotle's distinction between the passive and active faculties or *dunameis*.[22] Here, we will see that placing geometry with rhetoric means reading Aristotle against his psychologistic interpreters (George Kennedy and William Covino, to name only two) and recognizing the passive faculty as rhetoric's anchor in the realm of particularity, which Aristotle believed was outside of psychological conception or philosophical systematization. Rhetoric, in this way, becomes a response to the imperative of the particular; rhetoric is untotalized, yes, yet capable of formalization as an effect that has the structuration of a *dunamis* (faculty or possibility or potential).

Chapter 3, "Lacan and the Question of Rhetoric," is one possible response to the following question: If the province of rhetoric is the question, and the question is not mapped on the slope of ontology (in other words, rhetoric is an "unrealized"), how is one able to talk about what rhetoric *is*? In his "Agency [l'instance] of the Letter in the Unconscious," Lacan wonders whether a person can really think of rhetorical figures as simply figures of speech, since the figures themselves seem to be an active "participant" (what in Greek is called a *dunamis*?) in the analytic session. And it is for this reason that Shoshana Felman (a pupil first of Lacan, then of de Man) believes Lacan attempted to grammaticalize rhetoric and rhetoricize grammar in order to "speak" the unconscious by peeling tropes away from it. But, as Ellie Ragland-Sullivan has pointed out, Lacan's "dream of grammaticalizing or formalizing rhetoric became an impossibility when he realized that there is no privileged point of distance from language within language; no metalanguage; no Other of the Other" (*Jacques Lacan and The Philosophy of Psychoanalysis* 233). This is not to say, however, that rhetoric does not exist for Lacan nor even that Lacan's contribution to rhetoric is peculiar to an early phase of his work. In fact, I would argue that rhetoric again becomes useful for Lacan and that Lacan does, indeed, provide a formalization of rhetoric even though he might have failed to "grammaticalize" it. In his structural period (the early 1970s), rhetoric is formalized as an *adunamis* by Lacan—an impossibility or impotence operating within the four discourse structures he adumbrates in *Seminar XX* and *Seminar XVII*. To do so, let me remark, is not to allegorize rhetoric nor even to make of it a positivizable negative. Rather, rhetoric becomes the trajectory (slope) of a very particular aim, a shot—if you will—across a gap, within being and knowing via the signifiers of language. Rhetoric is a shot whose lack of realization evokes, in its discontinuity, the unconscious in the form of a question left over from the closure of words and sentences, "What is it you want, really?"[23] The relation of rhetoric and geometry appears in the form of a type of vector analysis with which Lacan makes possible the specification of these rhetorical trajectories and as well the slopes of metaphor and metonymy that have as their counterparts the derivatives by which a Lacanian calculus can determine the "instance of the letter" on the slope of the signifier and on the *objet* a.

In sum, Aristotle provides us with a space for rhetoric, and Lacan provides us with its place. Aristotle, in his conception of rhetoric as a *dunamis*, understood that rhetoric was not psychology, philosophy, ethics, or any other science; rhetoric consists of what has dropped out of the symbolization of each of those genres of inquiry. And, what is even more insightful, Aristotle assigned a particular construction (a particular space) to rhetoric as an unrealized psychology, an unrealized ethics, an unrealized politics, that is, rhetoric as the space in which an imperative demands one get up in the morning and negotiate the active and passive principles of the world, at least as Aristotle conceived of it. Lacan, likewise, conceived of rhetoric as an unrealized, but as a question—or better yet the mark of a question—indicating the persistence of a gap between an utterance and its enunciation.

Such work as Aristotle's and Lacan's will be of use in the promotion of rhetorical and interdisciplinary work in the academy, since no matter what degree of insight might be attributed to their formalizations of rhetoric, Aristotle's and Lacan's work on rhetoric—it must be admitted—is an example of what might be termed, *interdisciplinary study*. More important, theirs is as well an interdisciplinary study with, nonetheless, very particular structural consistencies (the interrogative and the imperative) that the following chapters will have specified if only in terms of their own interdisciplinary examination of the spaces and places for rhetoric in the work of two of its greatest theorists.

ARISTOTLE'S IMPERATIVE
FOR RHETORIC

If you consult Aristotle, everything
[about *jouissance*] will be made clear to
you

—Lacan, *Seminar XX: Encore*

Among rhetoricians, it is commonly held that Aristotle thought of rhetoric as an intellectual science while the Sophists, among others, argued rhetoric was merely an art. In fact, Aristotle's "let rhetoric be a faculty" has almost been a battle cry for those who wish to promote the study of rhetoric as a multidisciplinary yet an autonomous course of study. I wonder, though, if rhetoricians have taken advantage of what Aristotle's simple statement about rhetoric makes available to them, since, up to this point, no rhetorician has studied the use of the term *dunamis* throughout Aristotle's "philosophical system."

In this chapter, I will present a reading of *dunamis* in terms of what Aristotle has called its principal definition: "a being qua other," that is, reading *dunamis* as a phenomenon. However, I will also attempt, in the second section of this chapter, to demonstrate how this being qua other is more a structural than a phenomenological construct. I will address *dunamis* as a timing rather than as a being, insofar as Aristotle (among other things) describes the epideictic, deliberative, and forensic rhetorics in terms of their unique relationships to time. This discussion of the distinct relations of the three rhetorics to time will then lay the groundwork for discussion of the relation between Aristotle's references to the *dunamis* of rhetoric and to the *dunamis* of geometry. Geometry might then be placed *with* rhetoric rather than instead of rhetoric, thus countering the use of geometry to dismiss rhetoric—a dismissal which, in chapter 1, I identified in terms of the genealogical and onomastic moves of philosophy. In addition, by these means, I hope to place Aristotle *with* Lacan—seeing in both a philosophically informed rhetoric, but a nonphilosophical rhetoric nonetheless.

RHETORIC AS A FACULTY

My primary concern, at this first stage of my reading, is to understand what Aristotle could have meant when he wrote that rhetoric is a faculty (a *dunamis*), given that the word *dunamis* figures prominently in both his *Rhetoric* and his *Metaphysics*. Is there, then, some connection among Aristotle's various uses of *dunamis*? What is more, does the polysemy of the term argue for or against those who would speak of Aristotle's "philosophical rhetoric" or his "rhetorical philosophy"? Indeed, would such phrases as "philosophical rhetoric" and "rhetorical philosophy" have any meaning for Aristotle?

Unfortunately, one immediately begins to run into difficulties when trying to examine the relation of metaphysics and rhetoric in Aristotle's philosophy. It is difficult not to imagine that Aristotle, as a native speaker of ancient Greek, created absolutely unique instances of the word *dunamis* in his individual discussions of rhetoric and metaphysics. To have functioned as a working language, however, ancient Greek must have been both iterable and intentional. For this reason, I can say that, on the one hand, Aristotle no doubt thought of metaphysics and rhetoric as two distinct types of inquiry and, on the other, Aristotle's use of *dunamis* in the *Rhetoric* informs his use of the word in the *Metaphysics*—if only insofar as rhetoric is a thing which does, in fact, exist in the

Aristotelian "system." And it is precisely this simple quantification of rhetoric's existence that is so elusive to modern historians of rhetoric—even historians from such diverse backgrounds as the classicist George Kennedy and the poststructuralist William Covino.[1]

Kennedy's summary of Aristotle's views has been particularly popular among rhetoricians because he places rhetoric among the theoretical sciences (mathematics, metaphysics, and physical science). Kennedy argues that rhetoric must be, in some sense, theoretical for Aristotle, since the object of rhetoric is to know (*theorizein*) the available means of persuasion in any given situation (Kennedy 62). Kennedy does not take into account the fact that, for Aristotle, it is what each science purports to know that distinguishes it from another, not the fact that each has "knowledge" (of some kind) as its goal. That is, Kennedy assumes rhetoric is theoretical simply because it has, as a mode of inquiry, an object of knowledge. This is not the case for Aristotle. When Aristotle addresses the topic of the theoretical, practical, and productive sciences in the *Metaphysics*, he writes of the types of "substance" that each science investigates. Aristotle argues, for example, that physical science must be speculative or theoretical because it deals "with the sort of substance which contains in itself the principle of motion or rest" (1025b19–24). Thus, to determine what kind of "science" rhetoric is, according to Aristotle, will require that we investigate what sort of object rhetoric investigates.

Can we, then, following this program, expect to find in the *Rhetoric* a discussion of a type of substance uniquely suited to rhetoric? Yes and No. Rhetoric is a problematic subject for Aristotle, since rhetoric, as he sees it, does not have a definite subject matter. Aristotle argues that rhetoric is "a combination of the science of the logical and of the ethical branch of politics; and is partly like dialectic, partly like sophistical reasoning" (1359b8–10). For that reason, Aristotle complains, "rhetoric has been given a far wider subject matter than strictly belongs to it" (1359b7). Part of Aristotle's goal, then, in the *Rhetoric* is to define rhetoric as a subject matter that does not itself encompass any single, discrete subject. But Aristotle will have his cake, and he will eat it too.

On the one hand, rhetoric does have a subject matter—proofs. On the other hand, its own "existence" as a *dunamis* puts it in a precarious position with reference to proof.

The problem of definition that rhetoric represents for Aristotle has a parallel, interestingly enough, in chapter 3 of Book IX of the *Metaphysics*. "There are some people," Aristotle writes, "who say, as the Megaric school does, that a thing 'can' act only when it is acting, and when it is not acting it 'cannot' act, e.g. that he who is not building cannot build but only he who is building; and so in all other cases. It is not hard to see the absurdities that attend this view" (1046b28–33). Aristotle finds the view of the Megaric School "absurd" because "if that which is deprived of potency is incapable, that which is not happening will be incapable of happening" (1047a10–11). In other words, if the Megaric School denies potentiality/potency then it "does away with both movement and becoming," both of which Aristotle sees happening all around him.[2] Actually, it is not so much that those of the Megaric School deny potentiality as it is that they conflate potentiality with actuality; they believe that to have the potentiality to build a house, a person must be building a house. Aristotle, I believe, would see a similar conflation in the thinking of those who, like George Kennedy, would try to define rhetoric as a theory or a science simply because rhetoric can make (some sort of) claim to knowledge. And Aristotle argues as much: "But the more we try to make either dialectic or rhetoric not, what they really are, practical faculties, but sciences, the more we shall inadvertently be destroying their true nature, for we shall be re-fashioning them and shall be passing into the region of sciences dealing with definite subjects rather than simply with words and forms of reasoning" (1059b14–18). Here, Aristotle treats rhetoric as if it were little more than a set of decorations for thoughts about any given subject. Is such an adequate summary of Aristotle's thinking about rhetoric? I don't believe so, and neither does Kennedy. In fact, one might see in Kennedy's description of rhetoric as a theoretical science an attempt to obviate such a conclusion.

However, if we are to take Aristotle at his word, the crucial difference between the Megaric School and Aristotelian definitions of rhetoric is that Aristotle does not argue rhetoric is a means of persuasion; rather, it is, for him, a way to discover how to persuade in any given instance. Rhetoric is the presumption, not the assumption, of the possibility of persuasion. Whereas some philosophers would deny that there might be a possibility for persuasion when persuasion is not taking place, Aristotle—who argues in his *Metaphysics* that for there to be "movement and becoming" in this world there must be potentiality (*dunamis*)—can argue that if there is such a thing as persuasion then there must be such a thing as a potentiality (*dunamis*) for persuasion:

> Rhetoric then may be defined as the faculty [*dunamis*] of discovering [*theoreisai*] the available means [*endexomenon*] of [*pithanon*] in reference to any subject whatever. This is the function of no other of the arts, each of which is able to instruct and persuade in its special subject; thus, medicine deals with health and sickness, geometry with the properties of magnitudes, arithmetic with number, and similarly with all the other arts and sciences. But rhetoric, so to say, appears to be able to discover the means of persuasion in reference to any given subject. That is why we say that as an art its rules are not applied to any particular definite class of things. (1355b26–36)

I hesitate to call this simply a definition of rhetoric, since in both the English and the Greek, Aristotle does not write that "rhetoric *is* the faculty of observing." Rather, the imperative form of the verb "to be" translates as "let rhetoric be the faculty," or as Freese renders it, "rhetoric may be defined." Other commentators on the *Rhetoric* have made much of Aristotle's use of the imperative here, seeing in it something of the general hesitancy of the *Rhetoric*. Some have even argued that Aristotle's *Rhetoric* is itself rhetorical because Aristotle's tentative "let it be" treatment of the subject places the *Rhetoric* itself in the realm of the probable. Certainly, the imperative form of the verb is not the sort of construction Aristotle uses for definitions in his other works. Take, for example, the definition of *dunamis* that appears in the *Metaphysics*: "Potency means [*legetai*]: the source of motion or change which is in something other than the thing changed, or in it qua other" (12109z15–16).

Because of the use of *legetai*, it might be said that in terms of his metaphysics Aristotle is merely an observer/speaker who is only attempting to understand how the world about him goes along its merry way.[3] Of course, we might ask this humble Aristotle why *dunamis* means what he says it does, but I fear his reply would only be that "*dunamis legetai*—faculty/capacity/potentiality is said to be the source [*archeis*] of motion or change [*kineiseos e metaboleis*]."

The use of "let rhetoric be," on the other hand, does not put Aristotle in such a "neutral" position. That is, he doesn't seem to be merely observing how rhetoric has been defined so much as he is deciding how rhetoric might be defined. The responsibility that Aristotle assumes in the *Rhetoric* may explain the hesitant tone that some commentators have seen throughout that work (above rhetoric only "appears to be able to discover"). Even Aristotle's description of the relation of rhetoric and dialectic, according to this view, has a tentativeness about it; after all, rhetoric is only sort of an offshoot [*paraphues ti*] or sort of a part (*morion ti*) of dialectic.

But what such commentators have not explored is what it means to say rhetoric is a *dunamis*, that it is an existent qua other. Surely, Aristotle is neither tentative nor unsure about rhetoric here but is specifying rhetoric as something that does not have a simple referent any more than a recipe for a chocolate cake does.

For that reason, to understand Aristotle's rhetoric is not simply to understand what object is rhetoric's reference but to understand as well what type of existence rhetoric refers to. William Covino comes close to this realization about Aristotle in his self-described "revisionist history" of rhetoric: "One immobilizes rhetoric [Aristotle's rhetoric] by converting it from a habit of mind to a body of data, discouraging the collection of perspectives which—taken together—reveal the ambiguity and maintain the uncertainty [inherent in language] which creates more rhetoric" (25).

Although I may agree with the intent of Covino's "revisionist" interpretation of Aristotle's rhetoric, I can't see how Covino provides a reading of Aristotle here. First of all, Aristotle would not argue it is the ambiguity of language that makes the writing of a rhetoric necessary. In the first chapter of Book One of the *Rhetoric*, he writes it is the inability of some people to comprehend instruction that makes rhetoric necessary. Indeed, Aristotle, I believe, would have been very surprised to find out that language was inherently ambiguous.[4]

I also wonder if Aristotle thought of rhetoric as a "habit of mind," as Covino suggests. Granted, Aristotle does mention in the very first section of his *Rhetoric* that rhetoric and dialectic are things in which "all men in a manner have a share" because "all, up to a certain point, endeavor to criticize or uphold an argument, to defend themselves or to accuse. Now, the majority of people do this either at random or with a familiarity arising from habit" (1354a2). But is all this the same as arguing that rhetoric is a "habit of mind"? The Greek speaks of a *suneitheian eks hexios*, an ordinary occurrence arising from habit. If anything, the ability to criticize or uphold an argument is a *suneitheian* from habit, not the habit itself. The phrase "at random" is Freese's translation of *eikei tauta drosin*, meaning "this thing done without a plan or schedule." Nowhere do I see anything that would indicate rhetoric is a habit of mind, as Covino argues. In fact, we might see in the paragraph above yet another attempt on Aristotle's part to define rhetoric as a *dunamis* or potency free from twentieth-century psychologism. Yet, Covino's reading is understandable. Covino would like to cover over the contradictory nature of Aristotle's notion of rhetoric by rendering it as a "habit of mind." As a *suneithan eks hexios*, rhetoric would be related both to disorder (something done without plan) and order (a particular ordering from habit). Covino would like to assume that since the existence of rhetoric is not specified in terms of its object (that is, to know, according to Kennedy) the existence of rhetoric might be expressed in terms of its subject (that is, a habit of mind). In this manner, both Covino and Kennedy grasp one half of the problem, though neither is able to come to terms with the dual nature of Aristotle's proposed solution.

This point about the dual nature of Aristotle's rhetoric is further clarified when we observe how the notion that something might be done either at random or from that which is "accustomed from habit" nicely corresponds to the two types of potencies (*du-nameis*) one finds described in the *Metaphysics*: "As all potencies are either innate, like the senses, or come by practice, like the power of playing the flute, or by learning, like artistic power, those which come by practice or by rational formula we must acquire by previous experience but this is not necessary with those which are not this nature and which imply passivity" (1946b32–34). I assume the type of potency that is "innate" (*suggeneis*) and that implies "passivity" roughly corresponds to the ability to argue, which Aristotle says people acquire "at random." The other kind of potency comes from "practice [*matheisei*] or by rational formula [*technon*]." I would think that this "active" potency might be equivalent to the *suneitheian eks hexios* Aristotle speaks of above. For that reason, if I were to be asked if Aristotle thought rhetoric were something to be "learned" or something "innate," I might answer that, insofar as rhetoric is a *dunamis*, it is both "learned and innate."

At this point, we need to be careful not to assume that because a *dunamis* is "learned and innate" we can think of Aristotle's rhetoric as purely psychological. That is the mistake Kennedy makes by stressing the rational aspect of rhetoric (rhetoric as knowledge about something) and the mistake Covino makes by stressing the irrational aspect of rhetoric (rhetoric as something about which one might have knowledge).

The following examples of the two types of *dunameis*, from the *Metaphysics* should help clarify Aristotle's use of the term for us: "Potency means (1) a source of movement or change, which is in another thing than the thing moved or in the same thing qua other; e.g., the science of building is a potency which is not present in the thing built; but the science of medicine which is a potency, may be present in the patient, although not qua patient" (1019a15–18). The use of the science of medicine as an example is interesting to note here because Aristotle contrasted the faculty of rhetoric with the art of medicine. Medicine, it seems, has a more specific subject matter than rhetoric does and even has its own suasive power. Aristotle's rhetoric, in this way, is radically different from the rhetorics that came before it. Gorgias or Isocrates, for example, would have thought persuasion itself to be the province of rhetoric, so that if a doctor were able to persuade a patient to take streptomycin as a treatment for ulcerous lesions, she would do so only insofar as she had practiced the art of rhetoric; the art of medicine might have provided the cure, but the art of rhetoric provided the physician with the ability to convince her patient to take the cure. For Aristotle, each faculty—with the glaring exception of rhetoric—enables a person to both instruct and persuade others with reference to the subject matter of the respective faculty. We can appreciate the problem Aristotle sets himself up for here. If rhetoric does not have a specific subject, then how can it be identified as something discrete from any other *techne* or faculty?

I think Aristotle provides us with an answer to this question in the section from the *Metaphysics* cited above where he argues that some faculties are present in the actions of which they are the source and some are not. Indeed, Aristotle makes a similar point in the *Rhetoric*:

> It is thus evident that rhetoric does not deal with any one definite class of subjects, but, like Dialectic, [is of general application]; also, that it is useful; and further, that its function is not so much to persuade, as to find out in each case the existing means of persuasion. The same holds good in respect to all the other arts. For instance, it is not the function of medicine to restore a patient to health, but only to promote this end as far as possible; for even those whose recovery is impossible may be properly treated. (1355b9–18)

The introduction of the term *art*, or *techne*, need not further complicate the discussion of *dunamis*. But first one must realize that, for Aristotle, all *technai* are *dunameis*: "Since some such originate sources are present in soulless things, and others in things possessed of soul, and in the rational part of the soul, clearly some potencies will be non-rational and some will be accompanied by a rational formula. This is why all arts, i.e., all productive forms of knowledge, are potencies; they are originative sources of change in another thing or in the artist himself considered as other" (1046a37–1046b5).

Clearly, those who would argue that Aristotle's rhetoric is purely psychological would have trouble explaining Aristotle's association of *techne* with *dunamis*. Their exclusion of the technical from Aristotle's conception of rhetoric is, I think, a result of an attempt to solve, in a non-Aristotelian fashion, the problem of defining a *techne* or *dunamis* that has no specific subject matter. If rhetoric is purely psychological, they think, then it is an art of perception that is capable of taking any subject within its purview. The following from an article published in *Freshman English News* nicely summarizes this prevailing misconception:

> Gorgias and the pre-Socratic philosophers describe rhetoric as a *techne*, an art or craft of discourse-making, while Aristotle defines it as a *dynamis* or faculty—that is, an inherent human capacity. For many in our profession this division remains. To teach writing solely as craft is to grant preeminent values to the artistry of a finished product; to value the psychological aspect, in contrast, is to teach writing as "process" or an exercise of a faculty. (Baumlin and French-Baumlim 2)[5]

But Aristotle does not argue that all *dunameis* are purely "psychological." As we've just seen above, Aristotle distinguished between two kinds of faculties made distinct according to whether or not they are in things that have a soul. Those potencies that are not in things devoid of soul are called "nonrational"; those potencies that do exist in things with souls are "accompanied by a rational formula." This distinction between rational and nonrational *dunameis* seems to parallel as well the distinction we have already noted between the faculty of building and the faculty of medicine.

Indeed, observe the trouble one gets into when a person ignores the presence of the nonrational or passive faculty in Aristotle's conception of a *dunamis*. If one were to imagine two master builders, each assigned to build a house out of a different material, but one is asked to use reinforced concrete as a building material and the other is asked to use a tasty spinach pasta. Surely, it would not then be very kind to make a judgment of the relative abilities of the builders based on the resilience of their creations. There is such a thing, one must remember, as a passive faculty, that is, the ability of something to have action performed on it. A patient may have the ability to be treated medically, but I believe Aristotle would say that the tasty spinach pasta does not have the passive ability to be a building but that it has the passive ability to be eaten.

Thus, a *dunamis* cannot be purely psychological for Aristotle.

And Aristotle's rhetoric cannot be purely psychological. For one thing, this distinction between the passive and the active faculty may correspond to the difference between artificial and inartificial proof. Inartificial proof would parallel the passive faculty because it has the ability to be used as proof. Artificial proof, on the other hand, does not exist as proof outside the rhetor's production, so it would correspond to the rational aspect of *dunamis*. And Aristotle does seem to posit some relation between the two kinds of *dunameis* and two kinds of proof: "The modes of persuasion are the only true constituents of the art: everything else is merely accessory, since enthymemes are the substance of rhetorical persuasion" (1354a14–17).

Rhetoric does appear to have a subject matter of sorts—the enthymeme. But enthymemes are not subjects as Kennedy described earlier. That is, we do not need to imagine that rhetoric is a theoretical science to provide it with the enthymeme as a subject matter. Nor do we need to speak of rhetoric as a "habit of mind," as Covino does, to answer the question, "In what sense, does Aristotelian rhetoric exist given that it is a *dunamis*?" We simply must recognize in Aristotle's system a respect for the object as a nonpredicable, a respect for what is not psychological or what exists outside of some perceptual field. The "thing," for Aristotle, is not simply something to be acquired by our perception, but (insofar as we can know something about it as a *dunamis*) it is as well a "being qua other," with which we transact to create our perceptions and, therefore, the evidence (the signs and probabilities of enthymemes) for and of our existence. In this manner, Aristotle's metaphysics may be said to be rhetorical and his rhetoric metaphysical.

However, this is not to say Aristotle's understanding of being is limited to the ontological and metaphysical. For Aristotle's specification of the existence of rhetoric as a *dunamis* introduces time into the discussion of being; a *dunamis*, after all, is a potentiality, an anticipation of certainty as well as a power. To say that rhetoric, in some fashion, exists in the other or has a being qua other is to make a distinction between that being that is said (*legetai*) to exist and that type of being that, as an imperative, is said in order to exist. In the next section of this chapter, I will investigate in what fashion rhetoric might be said to be as an other—in what fashion rhetoric might be said (in order) to exist. My argument will be that such an existence is not a being as such but a being qua timing, hence, Aristotle's association of the three types of rhetoric with three different times (past, present, and future). Indeed, I will argue that it is by his association of the three types of rhetoric to their timings that Aristotle avoids the category error Lacan argues (in *Seminar XI*) is constitutive of philosophy: associating existence with meaning and knowledge without the intermediary cuts of desire. Lacan said this in a different way in "L'instance de la lettre," as I will explain in chapter 3: philosophy provides no explanation for the fact that metaphor is associated with being and metonymy with its lack. And rhetoric, as Aristotle conceived of it, begins to.

RHETORIC, TIME, AND THE GEOMETRY OF DESIRE

In the previous section of this chapter, I used Aristotle's discussion of faculties and potentialities in the *Metaphysics* to specify what he might have meant when he said that rhetoric was a faculty or potentiality. I would like to extend that discussion by examining, in a tangential fashion, Aristotle's use of the imperative *esto* in his definition of rhetoric. Examining Aristotle's use of the imperative, I will argue, establishes the rationale for his specification of the enthymeme as the object and the problematic of rhetorical inquiry. Certainly, the determination of truth values for imperatives has been a source of great difficulties for logicians and philosophers of ethics.[6] In the seventeenth century, a number of English poets desperately tried to provide a logic with which they might command, with some sense of necessity, "Seize the day".[7] But I will argue that Aristotle's interest in the imperative mood is more an example of what he saw to be a problem with all propositions, that is, their specification in terms of some temporal operator. Such an assertion is consistent with the work that has already been done on how Aristotle associates the problem of assigning truth values to imperative propositions with the problem of assigning truth values to ethical propositions positing some truth about "what a person should do in the future."[8] In fact, I would see both ethics and rhetoric to be the repositories for what escapes formalization in terms of the particular logical structures of Aristotelian science: "There is not truth or falsity in all sentences; a prayer is a sentence which is neither true or false. The present investigation [his *On Interpretation*] deals with the statement-making sentence. The others we can dismiss, since consideration of them belongs rather to the study of rhetoric or poetry" (17a3–6).

To escape formalization, I might say even, is one of Aristotle's definitions of *dunamis*: "Matter exists in a potential state, just because it may attain to its form; and when it exists actually, then it is in its form" (1051a11). To be actualized, according to Aristotle, is to have form; potentiality lacks form but has a potential for it. One cannot, however, jump to the conclusion that rhetoric is not formalizable. On the contrary, Aristotle formalizes rhetoric as that which has the potential for being formalized; Aristotle's insight into the ontological and epistemological status of rhetoric is that rhetoric *is* something that always *will be* formalized. Truly, in the Aristotelian sense of the word, rhetoric is a *thing*; it is *now* in the making (as opposed to ethics that *will be* in the making). For this reason, what Aristotle offers in his rhetorical theory is an imperative, a "Let rhetoric be." As I intend to show, this imperative marks the relation between the way different moments of time are actualized by becoming identified with the eternally identical "now." *This is Aristotle's imperative for rhetoric.* To extend an argument of Jaako Hintikka's, this imperative marks "the way in which the content of a known 'now' statement becomes relevant to the word at the different moments of time by becoming utterable at the moment in question" (47).

I stress *the now*, at the onset, since it is the problematic of *the now*, the problem *the now* presents to a logic, that both geometry and rhetoric are designed to address, as Aristotle sees it. But before I speak further about the relation of geometry and rhetoric to *the now*, let me indicate what I see as two instances of Aristotle's struggle with the logical formulation of *the now*:

> 1. For the same statement [*logos*] seems to be both true and false. Suppose, for example, that the statement that somebody is sitting is true; after he has got up this statement will be false.

Similarly with beliefs. Suppose you believe truly that somebody is sitting; after he has got up you will believe falsely if you hold the same belief about him. (4a23–8)

2. Statements and beliefs, on the other hand, themselves remain completely unchangeable in every way; it is because the actual thing changes that the contrary comes to belong to them. For the statement that somebody is sitting remains the same; it is because of a change in the actual thing that it comes to be true at one time and false at another. Similarly with beliefs. (4a34–4b2)

Aristotle's idea of "changing truth" has to be distinguished from the modern idea of the historical relativity of truth. A historical relativist or social constructivist will argue for the impossibility of obtaining truths resistant to the vagaries of truth criteria. Aristotle, however, was not concerned with changes in our criteria of truth, but changes in the objects truths are about. He was not concerned with changes in a person's notions about reality, but with changes in the reality itself. As Hintikka points out, "Aristotle did not think that the discovery of truth is usually very difficult; the difficulty was, rather, that all the truths concerning changing things had to be found (as it were) all over again at each new moment" (45). Or, in the words of Aristotle:

It is not because we think that you are white, that you are white, but because you are white we who say this have the truth. If, then, some things are always combined and cannot be separated, and others are always separated and cannot be combined, while others are capable either of combination or of separation, being is being combined and one, and not being is being not combined but more than one; regarding contingent facts, then, the same opinion or the same statement comes to be false and true, and it is possible at one time to have the truth and at another to be in error; but regarding things that cannot be otherwise opinions are not at one time true and at another false, but the same opinions are always true or always false. (786a–96)

The problem of establishing the truth value of *the now* is not simply that it is always changing, since one of those things "that cannot be otherwise," in Aristotle's thinking, is *the now*. Indeed, Aristotle will argue that *the now* is itself a *tode ti*, a "this":

The "now" corresponds to the body that is carried along, as time corresponds to the motion for it is by means of the body that is carried along that we become aware of the before and after in the motion, and if we regard these as countable we get the "now." Hence in these also the "now" as substratum remains the same (for it is what is before and after in movement), but its being is different; for it is in so far as the before and after is that we get the now. This is what is most knowable, for motion is known because of that which is moved, locomotion because of that which is carried. For what is carried is a "this," the movement is not [*tode gar ti to feromenon ei de kineisis ou*]. Thus the "now" in one sense is always the same, in another it is not the same; for this is true also of what is carried. (219b22–33)

If one remembers that Aristotle defined potentiality as the cause of motion, this passage provides an analogy situating rhetoric quite nicely within the problematics of Aristotle's physics and metaphysics. Aristotle, here as well, avoids the conflation of relation and cause that marks genealogical and onomastic philosophical thought. It is not enough to say that by situating rhetoric as a *dunamis* Aristotle introduces into his rhetorical theory the problematic relation of the before and the after that constitutes *the now*. For as Lacan's derivation of the object $\underline{a}$ in terms of the instant/instance of the letter shows (see chapter 3), relationality can constitute causality. But rather than define this relationality in terms of the locus of incorporation (as Lacan does), Aristotle specifies it in terms of the corporal itself.

The problem of *the now*, in this light, is akin to the problem of establishing a logically derived definition for the body. Both *the now* and the body are particulars—that to which a demonstrative "this" might be assigned. But the contradictory nature of the two becomes apparent from an Aristotelian point of view at the moment one considers either to be countable or not countable; the now, for example, is a countable body. When Aristotle says that the being of the body or the being of *the now* is different, he means that their being is known only in terms of the relation between the before and the after: what is more or less than the two. Paradoxically, the body and *the now* are the host for the similarities and sameness by which motion and time are perceived as differential structures. In fact, motion and time cannot be perceived separate from the body and *the now*—even though the body and *the now* can have what Aristotle called an existence separate from motion and time. That is what Aristotle means when he writes that *the now* and the body are "in one sense always the same, in another not the same." Separate from motion and time, they are not always the same; combined with motion and time, they are always the same. Aristotle, in this manner, turns inside out the problem of specifying truth values for temporally operative propositions. The problem of establishing a "truth-functional logic" of *the now* or a logic of the body, then, is an effect of treating the body and *the now* as separate from motion and time. But what does it mean not to separate the body from motion or *the now* from time? What sort of logic might that be?

Perhaps, Aristotle called enthymemes the *soma*, or body, of persuasion for good reason. It is in and around the heart—in one's body—that the *thymos* is found. And if, for Aristotle, the body correlates directly with enthymemes, then truth would correlate directly with desire—*epithumia*: "What affirmation and negation are in thinking, pursuit and avoidance are in desire; so that since moral virtue is a state of character concerned with choice, and choice is deliberate desire, therefore both the reasoning must be true and the desire right, if the choice is to be good, and the latter must pursue just what the former asserts. Now this kind of intellect and of truth is practical" (1139a21–27). For Aristotle, persuasion does not have as its aim that someone should give up on his or her desire; it is a structuring of desire as a deliberate choice between contradictions formally derived from a body, from *the now* and their relations to motion and time: "The demonstrative premise differs from the dialectical, because the demonstrative premise is the assertion of one of two contradictory statements (the demonstrator does not ask for his premises, but lays them down), whereas the dialectical premise depends on the adversary's choice between two contradictories" (24a21–24b10).

The role of choice in the construction of enthymemes creates its own problems for the rhetorician in as much as rhetorical texts are not dialectical ones; that is, rhetorical discourse needs to be cut into. Bitzer makes this point in his influential work on the enthymeme:

> The interaction between speaker and audience must have a different form in rhetoric, however, because continuous discourse by the speaker does not allow him or her to obtain premises from his or her audience through question and answer. The enthymeme is a syllogism based on probabilities, signs, and examples, whose function is rhetorical persuasion. Its successful construction is accomplished through the joint efforts of speaker and audience, and this is its essential character. (408)

The enthymeme, then, figures individual choice as social discourse. It materializes the gaps between what is said (*logos*), who says it (*ethos*), and what is heard behind what is said (*pathos*), using the truth value of *the now* as both the links and the limits of such a discourse.

Mark how these gaps (more in the sense of divisions really) introduce mathematics into Aristotle's rhetoric:

> The now is the link of time, as has been said (for it connects past and future time), and it is a limit of time (for it is the beginning of the one and the end of the other). But this is not obvious as it is with the point, which is fixed. It divides potentially, and in so far as it is dividing the "now" is always different, but in so far as it connects it is always the same, *as it is with mathematical lines*. For the intellect is not always one and the same point, since it is other and other when one divides the line; but in so far as it is one, it is the same in every respect. So the "now" also is in one way a potential dividing of time, in another the termination of both parts, and their unity. And the dividing and the uniting are the same thing and in the same reference, but in essence they are not the same. (222a10–20, emphasis mine)

When one recognizes that *the now* is both a link and a limit for the past and the future, it is understandable that when Aristotle associates three different types of rhetoric with three different times, epideictic rhetoric, which is associated with the now, is also concerned with the past and future:

Further, to each of these a special time is appropriate: to the deliberative the future, for the speaker, whether he exhorts or dissuades, always advises about things to come; to the forensic the past, for it is always in reference to things done that one party accuses and the other defends; to the epideictic most appropriately the present, for it is the existing condition of things that all those who praise or blame have in view. It is not uncommon, however, for epideictic speakers to avail themselves of other times, of the past by way of recalling it, or of the future by way of anticipating it. (1358b12–20)

Furthermore, the relation of rhetoric to geometrical reasoning becomes quite clear when one remembers how the imperative form was used in early geometries to specify what act of construction would establish the truth value of propositions about given geometrical objects in the *to nun*—in *the now*. Quite clearly, it is the very act of construction that is the proving ground for geometrical objects in Aristotle's thought:

It is by actualization also that geometricians are discovered; for it is by dividing the given figures that people discover them. If they had been already divided, the relations would have been obvious; but as it is the divisions are present only potentially. Why are the angles of the triangle equal to two right angles? Because the angles about one point are equal to two right angles. If then, the line parallel to the side had been already drawn, the theorem would have been evident for any one as soon as he saw the figure. Why is the angle in a semicircle in all cases a right angle? Because if three lines are equal—the two which form the base, and the perpendicular from the centre—the conclusion is evident at a glance to one who knows this premise. Obviously, there the potentially existing relations are discovered by being brought to actuality (the reason being that thinking is the actuality of thought); so that potentiality is discovered from actuality (and therefore it is by an act of construction that people acquire the knowledge), though the single actuality is later in generation. (1051a22–33)

In this manner, Aristotle responds to the problem of formalizing the particular. First, there is the opposition between the logical priority of the potential and the existential priority of the actual.

Knowledge is, in effect, knowledge about some thing for Aristotle. But the thing is placed on the side of the potential, that which has not come into its form. Knowledge, then, becomes a thing's formalization and actualization. This is not some *esse percipi est*, however. When one discovers the potential of some thing, one does not discover a set of truth conditions or historical circumstances; one discovers precisely the thingness of something. But since a thingness cannot be formalized, the act of construction, which has as its result the discovery of a thing, itself becomes our knowledge of the thing. Aristotle's notion of the object of construction is much more complicated than suggested by those who never grow tired of speaking and writing about Aristotle's good common sense. The object, for Aristotle, is not something that eats grass outside of one's window; it is not a cannonball dropped from a lopsided tower. In fact, Aristotle would put such things in the place of the particular and "no art has the particular in view."

> Medicine for instance [does not theorize about] what is good for Socrates or Callias, but what is good for this or that class of persons (for this is a matter that comes within the province of an art, whereas the particular is infinite and cannot be the subject of a true science). [And, for that reason] rhetoric will not consider what seems probable in each individual case, for instance to Socrates or Hippias, but that which seems probable to this or that class of persons. (1356b30–35)

In fact, "the happier a man is in his choice of propositions, the more he will unconsciously prove a science quite different from Dialectic and Rhetoric" (1321b14). To remain a rhetorician, a person must become content with his or her discontentment. More particularly, one must be content with the enthymeme as one's tool of investigation because it is by its means that the actual might become an object of inquiry if only insofar as the existence of the actual is a prerequisite for its own actualization in the construction of the potential.

> Each question will be best investigated in this way—by suppos-
> ing separate what is not separate, as the arithmetician and the

geometer do. For a man qua man is one indivisible thing: and the arithmetician supposes one indivisible thing, and then considers whether any attribute belongs to a man qua indivisible. But the geometer treats him neither qua man nor qua indivisible, but as a solid. For evidently the attributes which would have belonged to him even if he had not been indivisible can belong to him apart from these attributes. Thus, then, geometers speak correctly—they talk about existing things, and their subjects do exist; for being has two forms—it exists not only in fulfillment but also as matter. (1078a22–30)

The reason Aristotle allowed that geometers can, as he puts it, "speak correctly" is that for Aristotle geometrical demonstration always takes place in *the now* because it is in the act of construction (in the act of making separate what is not separate) that languages, mathematics included, have a referent.

Rhetoric, however, does deal with the particular in a way not available to geometry—since rhetoric by means of the enthymeme is concerned with the probable, and the probable is concerned with the particular but not as such: "It will become so owing to the probability being not probable absolutely but only in particular" (1402a15–16). Further, because Aristotle aligns the probable on the side of the particular, the probable has contradiction as one of its fundamental logical structures. I say that the probable has contradiction as one of its logical structures, since contradiction always allows for other possibilities. What is interesting about Aristotle's treatment of contradiction is that it does not engender any possibility whatsoever, as some neo-Aristotelian logics would have it. In fact, "any possibility" is not possible in Aristotelian terms, since potentiality delimits what can be said to be possible. Indeed, placed on the side of the particular that only exists potentially, contradiction is the guarantee of a limit for Aristotle: curiously, a limit to what cannot be said to exist.

After all, there is no limit to what can be said to exist actually. Aristotle makes that quite clear in his discussion of metaphor in the *Rhetoric*: "Homer often, by making use of metaphor, speaks of inanimate things as if they were animate; and it is to creating actuality in all such cases that his popularity is due . . . for he gives movement and life to all, and actuality is movement" (1412a 3–4).

This is not to say that poetry is grounded on the possibility of infinite extension. Quite the contrary, to pass out being to anything is an act of infinite extension (metaphor?), but to pass out nonbeing would be an act of infinite division (metonymy?). Why? Being is a less than one, Aristotle says; you can never have more than enough of it. Nonbeing is another matter; it is a more than one; you can have more than enough of it. Although Aristotle's point may be difficult to understand at first, it should be no surprise. There is an old academic chestnut that goes something like "the Greeks abhorred infinity." And what kind of infinity does Aristotle allow above? ONE that isn't ever more than enough. ONE that never goes too far. ONE you can take home to meet the folks. What kind of infinity does Aristotle not allow? ONE that "is" more than enough—$n + 1$. That is, if Nonbeing is an $n + 1$, it can serve as the actualization of an infinity, something Aristotle will not allow. Strictly speaking, Being seems not to fare much better in Aristotle's system than Nonbeing, since there is a kernel of non-possibility (Note: I do not say impossibility.) at the heart of Being. If Being is a less than one, one must admit that knowledge of it involves the positivization of an absolute negativity, a void (something that is never enough). Both the void and infinity only exist potentially in actuality and actually in knowledge:

The infinite [*to apeiron*] and the void [*to kenon*] and all similar things are said to exist potentially and actually in a different sense from that in which many other things are said so to exist, e.g. that which sees or walks or is seen. For of the latter class these predicates can at some time be truly asserted without qualification; for the seen is so called sometimes because it is being seen, sometimes because it is capable of being seen. But the infinite does not exist potentially in the sense that it will ever actually have separate existence [*hos energeia esomenon xoriston*]; its separateness is only in knowledge. For the fact that division never ceases to be possible gives the result that this actuality exists potentially, but not that it exists separately [*to de ksoridzesthai ou*]. (1048b10–17)

What does it mean to exist separately? To exist separately means to be defined without reference to motion and perceptibility (that is, without reference to matter):

> And since each of the sciences must somehow know the "what" and use this as a principle, we must not fail to observe how the natural philosopher should define things and how he must state the formula of the substance—whether as akin to snub or rather to concave. For of these the formula of the snub includes the matter of the thing, but that of the concave is independent of the matter; for snubness is found in a nose, so that its formula includes the nose—for the snub is a concave nose. (1064a29–26)

These considerations play an important role in Aristotle's theory of place. According to Aristotle, the place of an object is the "inner limiting surface of the body that contains" the object (212a7), this inner limit being a real physical subdivision. Hence, "if a thing is not separated from its embracing environment but continuous with it, it has a place as part of the whole" (211a29). Feyerabend explains this rather well:

> A bottle partly filled with water and floating in a lake has a place in the lake: the surface consists of the surface where the outside water meets the bottle—added to the surface where the outside air meets the bottle. The water inside the bottle also has a place, viz., the inner surface of the glass where it touches the inside water plus the surface of the inside air that touches the water. Both places are physically identifiable surfaces; however, a drop of water inside the bottle is part of that water; it has no place in that water; it has only, as part of that water, a place inside the bottle. We say that the droplet *potentially* has a place inside the water of the bottle and that this *potential* place can be *actualized* when the droplet is physically separated from the rest of that water, e.g., when it freezes (212b2). (222, emphases mine)

It is in terms of an object's place that one can see being separated as an act of actualization. What is actualized in separateness is the place of a thing. Thus, those things that always exist separately are never actualized as parts but always exist as potentialities (*dunameis*)—and curiously, not potentialities for themselves but for their places. Such a statement strikes at the heart of Aristotle's *Rhetoric* inasmuch as the enthymeme as the object of his rhetoric is actualized as a place (*chora*), which has as its corollary the movement (*kineisis*) of an audience member's mind: "One must therefore make room in the hearer's mind for the speech one intends to make" (*Rhetoric* iii.17.15). Persuasion, then, becomes a designation of the relation of place and motion in Aristotle's thinking.

Furthermore, Aristotle uses this distinction between "that which can be said to exist separately" and "that which cannot" to solve Zeno's paradox of Achilles and the tortoise. And here we will run into Aristotle's stopping place. Zeno observed that a movement over a certain distance must first cover half the distance, then half of the half and so on—with the result that the movement is never completed. In this paradox, Aristotle saw the assertion of two ways to divide movement. A person could divide the movement by using mathematical points but, in that event, no subdivision would have occurred. Or, the movement might be divided by using physical points, in essence changing it—turning it into an "incomplete" and "intermittent motion" (263a30).

But what kind of solution is that?! One can subdivide motion mathematically, which is to treat division as if it were not division—that is, treat division as if it were one—treat division itself as if it existed separately, existed only in knowledge. Or one can really divide motion; one can interrupt motion, cutting it temporally, and then the action is never completed but becomes another action that when really cut is itself interrupted and one starts all over again. It is almost as if Aristotle's "solution" to Zeno's paradox is to say Achilles and the tortoise never get off the mark.

Enter the prime mover that is itself unmoved. The place one might have assigned to Achilles and the tortoise above, Aristotle assigns to god, who is the form of form, the prime mover that is itself unmoved. And because god steps in and stays on the mark, Achilles and the tortoise can get set and go; they can have their fun; they can go on with the race. But where does that put Achilles and the tortoise? Quite frankly, they are cheaters—always starting a little ahead of the mark, always starting just a little before a gunshot or trumpet blast has started the race. That this is a problem of ethics is obvious; that this is a problem of rhetoric will need to be explained in chapters 3 and 4. Suffice it to say that, at this point, I do not believe my examination of the presuppositions for Aristotle's representation of the relation of rhetoric to geometry—which has as one of its ancillary propositions, "We're all cheaters"—heralds some revitalized descent into pluralism where everything might be said to be a game since life and death are presumed to be not at stake. Rather, I would see Aristotle's rhetoric as concerned with the call (the imperative) of desire [epithumia], just as Lacan's (as we will see in chapter 3) is concerned with desire as the question of being [l'instance de l'etre]. Chapter 4 will relate more specifically Aristotle's imperative and Lacan's question by way of Lacan's discussion of discourse, in particular "scientific discourse."[9]

3

LACAN AND THE
QUESTION OF RHETORIC

Periphrasis, hyperbaton, ellipsis, suspension, anticipation, re-
traction, negation, digression, irony, these are the figures of
style (Quintilian's *figurae sententiarum*); as catachresis, litotes,
antonomasia, hypotyposis are the tropes, whose terms suggest
themselves as the most proper for the labelling of these mecha-
nisms. Can one really see these as mere figures of speech when
it is the figures themselves that are the active principle of the
rhetoric of the discourse that the analysand in fact utters? (*Ecrits:
A Selection* 169)

Despite the extended reference to Quintilian, Lacan is thinking of rhetoric in more than tropological terms here. What
more Lacan has to say about rhetoric depends on how one
would read "the active principle" above. Is Lacan simply interested
in how language creates a subject? Perhaps, but it must be remem-
bered that the relation of the subject to language takes form, for
Lacan, as a question:

What I seek in speech is the response of the other. What constitutes me as subject is my question. In order to be recognized by
the other, I utter what was only in view of what will be. In order
to find him, I call him by a name that he must assume or refuse
in order to reply to me. (*Ecrits: A Selection* 86)

These considerations, important as their existence is for the
philosopher, turn us away from the locus in which language
questions us as to its very nature. And we will fail to pursue the

question further as long as we cling to the illusion that the signifier answers to the function of representing the signified, or better, that the signifier has to answer for its existence in the name of any signification whatever. (*Ecrits: A Selection* 150)

Lacan writes that language questions us about its nature. One way to understand a person's relation to language in Lacanian terms is to think precisely that, because of language, people are questions for themselves and for others; for example, "Am I alive or am I dead?" "Am I a man or am I a woman?" Lacan's very literal reliance on the form of the question is even more apparent in the famous *Che Vuoi* graph from the essay, "The Subversion of the Subject and the Dialectic of Desire."[1] But I am focusing my attention here on another of Lacan's essays, his "L'instance de la lettre dans l'inconscient," since in that essay Lacan makes some of his most overt references to rhetoric.

Lacan wrote "L'instance de la lettre" in what Jacques-Alain Miller has termed Lacan's phenomenological stage of thinking. My discussion of this essay in terms of rhetoric will take the form of a commentary on the Sheridan translation. A commentary seems the most suitable vehicle for an introduction to Lacanian rhetoric, since it will anchor the discussion, in very precise ways, to a widely available text. Furthermore, Lacan's work on metaphor and metonymy, when associated with his notion of rhetoric in that essay, will provide a structure I can then trace from Lacan's early phenomenological period to his later work. I attempt, in this manner, to construct a rhetoric that Lacan's work has specified but that is not, particularly in his "topological period," labeled as rhetoric per se.[2]

THE PHENOMENOLOGICAL STAGE OF LACAN'S THOUGHT

When I speak of a phenomenological stage in Lacan's conception of rhetoric, I do not mean that Lacan was a phenomenologist, nor do I mean that I can see the influence of Heidegger, Merleau-Ponty, or anyone else in Lacan's text at this time. I mean that at this period in time Lacan was learning something from phenomenology's recognition of the onto-epistemological assumptions of scientific discourse and from phenomenology's recognition that some-

51

thing which does not have existence as a predicate might be the object of scientific inquiry. I hope to show that this problematic coincides with Lacan's theorizing of the impossible in the seventies. But at this time in Lacan's writing, the fifties, there is a more noticeable interest in how the object of a scientific inquiry might be identified in terms other than (but not to the exclusion of) the categories of presence and absence.[3] In fact, that is how I would explicate the first half of Lacan's title, "L'instance de la lettre [l'être]": instance/agency as something that does not take up space even as an absence. And that is the challenge Lacan makes to the genealogical and onomastic moves of philosophy.

LACAN'S CHALLENGE TO THE ONOMASTIC

Possibility and the Question of Being

Early on in his career Lacan put into question a fundamental phenomenological precept: that possibility itself is something that moves beyond a question of presences or absences. Merleau-Ponty writes: "It must be shown that science is possible, that the sciences of man are possible, and that philosophy also is possible. The conflict between systematic philosophy and the advancing knowledge of science must cease" (228).

I find this citation from "Phenomenology and the Sciences of Man" particularly helpful when attempting to come to terms with what has been called Lacan's phenomenological stage. Phenomenology here is presented as an investigation of possibilities and the establishment of truth criteria for those possibilities. It may seem a bit curious—certainly a conflation of what in structuralist theory-building has been called a theory's "descriptive, explanatory, and predictive powers"—to establish the truth criteria for something that is already assumed to exist, if only as a possibility. But Lacan's own argument with phenomenology is that it is uninterested in what does not fall within the field of perception, that is, what is not constituted as a unitary relation between a subject and that subject's view of the world registered in relation to an other. Thus, Lacan argues that phenomenology focuses on possibilities because, phenomenologically speaking, the subject represents a place of growth for the other and vice versa, where one person establishes the truth conditions for the other. Hence, choice and decision are conceived by the phenomenologist as symbolic-order phenomena.[4]

Demand, Possibility, Merleau-Ponty, and the Question of Being

Lacan too is interested, at this stage in his thinking, in possibilities. More specifically, he is interested in the possibility of such a thing as psychoanalysis and its object of inquiry: the unconscious. But Lacan does not, even at this early stage in his thinking, ignore the function of impossibility, conceived at this time as the void.[5]

But before discussing the issue of impossibility, I would like to address an apparent similarity between phenomenological and Lacanian thought. Let us compare two statements, one by Merleau-Ponty and the other by Lacan—each delineating what might be called approaches to the "linguistic" and "ontological" status of the question.

Merleau-Ponty in 1967 [1968]:

But already when I say "what do I know?" in the course of a phrase, another sort of question arises: for it extends to the idea of knowing itself; it invokes some intelligible place where the facts, examples, ideas I lack, should be found; it intimates that the interrogative is not a mode derived by inversion or by reversal of the indicative and of the positive, is neither an affirmation nor a negation veiled or expected, but an original manner of aiming at something, as it were a question-knowing, which by principle no statement or "answer" can go beyond and which perhaps therefore is the proper mode of our relationship with Being, as though it were the mute or reticent interlocution of our questions. (*The Visible and the Invisible* 129)

Lacan in 1956:

The "being" referred to is that which appears in a lightning moment in the void of the verb "to be" and I said that it poses its question for the subject. What does that mean? It does not pose it before the subject, since the subject cannot come to the

53

place where it is posed, but it poses it in place of the subject, as one poses a problem with a pen, or as Aristotle's man thought with his soul. ("Agency [l'instance] of the Letter" 168)

It is no doubt tempting to list the similarities between the arguments presented in the two passages. I must remind myself at the onset, however, that by the time Merleau-Ponty wrote *The Visible and the Invisible* in the late sixties he had had much time to learn from what Lacan was saying in the seminars Merleau-Ponty had attended. As a matter of fact, in the English translation of his *The Visible and the Invisible*, the translator—Alphonso Lingis—has made note of at least one of Merleau-Ponty's borrowings from Lacan. There are even many American readers of Lacan who render his work as if it were phenomenology, but they are able to do so only by eliding the careful distinctions Lacan has made between demand and desire. Phenomenology cannot address the question of desire.

For Merleau-Ponty, as with Descartes, the "beyond" is conceived as a symbolic-order phenomenon, countable as one "beyond" at a time.[6] In fact, the beyond is represented here as its own possibility registered, in turn, as a question; no answer can go beyond this "beyond." The question, he tells us, "invokes" some "intelligible place" where what one lacks is materialized or positivized as such (as a lack). Yet, the question is not itself a lack, but a trajectory, an aim that quite literally gives shape to both our inquiries and their objects—linking our demands for what we lack to our Being. I say "demands" in this explication because Merleau-Ponty goes on to say that Being itself is question, albeit a mute one. Thus, Being ultimately resolves itself in terms of some symbolic order reduced to a signifier (in this case, a metaphor) for lack, "our relation to Being." Yes, our relation to Being is a lack, in these terms. And Merleau-Ponty's "question" may not be able to resolve itself as an answer, but it certainly does so as a demand.

It is not by chance that Slavoj Žižek uses the *Living Dead* movies as a means to elaborate Lacan's notion of demand. In terms of Lacan's understanding of demand, the phenomenological insistence on possibility as the existential category par excellence is seen to render life as death, life as a return of that which is foreclosed in a particular symbolic order. But what kind of life is that? Certainly not one that is worth living: if one is not properly buried, if the necessary obsequies have not been observed in terms of the symbolic, then life appears as a demand—for blood (in Vampire movies), for brains (in Zombie movies), or for some long-lost body/part (in the movies *Freejack*, *The Hand*).

What is more, the identification of questions with demands makes too little of the combinatory power of the symbolic, since there is no equivocation at the level of demand: demand is always the demand for one thing. Zombies, after all, know what they want. Brains. And they ask for it unequivocally. Brains. There is no such thing as unknown knowledge with reference to demand. Brains. Demand is, to use Merleau-Ponty's language, a question which extends "the idea of knowing itself." Brains. It is a formalization of the beyond but not as such—truly, a living death, life from/of the beyond, at least, knowledge dead on arrival. Brains.

Desire, Potentiality, Lacan, and the Question of Being

To the discussion of the question of being, Lacan adds the "void" and desire. Merleau-Ponty's assertion of the relation among possibility, a "beyond," and the question only tells half of the story from a Lacanian perspective. For Lacan, possibility is a dialectic consisting of two movements that he calls alienation and separation. One might call alienation the inscription of *the pure possibility* of the human subject as a place of demand within the symbolic order.[7] And one might think of separation as the inscription of the human subject as a *potential* object of desire. Lacan symbolizes both operations with the same punch sign or diamond [$\Diamond$] that is used to signify "possibility" in some notation systems. Yet, in its Lacanian orientation, the bottom half of the diamond represents the vel ($\vee$ used to signify "or" in symbolic logic) of alienation; the upper half of the punch represents the Scheffer's stroke ($\wedge$ used to signify "nor" in symbolic logic) of separation. Lacan's reading of the modal operator for possibility is more than playful; he does not want us to forget that alienation and separation constitute two orders of choice: alienation (either/or); separation (neither/nor). A brief dis-

55

cussion of these two orders of choice will help to explicate Lacan's particular contribution to the discussion on the relation of questions to knowing and being, since the question of desire is precisely what the logic of separation (neither this nor that) chisels in the face of being.

ALIENATION

For Lacan, instrumentality (for example, "as one poses a problem with a pen") and accompaniment ("as Aristotle's man thought with his soul") are the two "choices" for "being"—choices that are presented as locatives in place of the subject and as choices that are "substitutions for" rather than "hypostitizations of" being. Choice, in these terms, is a matter of substituting one thing for the other (*either* this *or* that) because loss itself cannot be symbolized. Granted, Lacan says there is a void within "to be." But this void manifests itself as a "moment" within which being might ask its question as the timing of the human subject. Elsewhere, this "timing of the human subject" is called a "hontologie," a guiltology, a be(hold)ing. According to Lacan, everybody has debts they cannot pay because the survival of the species requires what Johnson (contrary to Darwin) in his *Rasselas* called "the choice of life." In *Seminar XI*, Lacan describes this kind of choice as follows: when someone demands your money or your life, you have to choose life unless you would care to lose both your money and your life.[8] Then, how can one ever pay off a debt or live on anything other than borrowed time? How can this possibility for life or growth ever be actualized, ever be more than a want-to-be and not merely an unreasonable demand for life? Such is the forced choice of alienation.

To move from alienation to separation (from demand to desire) requires that one recognize in this forced choice of alienation not only the conceptualization of choice as a bifurcation but the conceptualization of bifurcation itself as a choice, a mark of an act of substitution (always in the past perfect) that positivizes loss as its contiguity—a contiguity, around which Lacan rethinks metonymy, desire, and the body (as we will discover in my discussion of metaphor and metonymy later). Loss, then, subtends the symbolic order; it is a nonsensical excess—a growth, if you will, on the symbolic order. This is not to say that "loss is what the Other lacks." No, the "beyond" of loss is not positivized in the Other in these terms. Rather, the Other itself is found lacking and the human subject becomes its potential object of desire. Lacan never tires from saying, "Desire is the desire of the Other."

SEPARATION

an excursus on *jouissance*, desire, and a few other Lacanian terms that I should probably define

---

The subject's response, the subject's re-joinder because of inherent loss, is *the question* of the subject itself as a desiring being: What do I want (what do you want of me), really? This question of desire, however, is not contiguous with the human subject (having to do with *jouissance* as a cause in the drives). The question of desire is a substitute for the subject who is contiguous with the gap between being and subject, which, in turn, poses the question of being. There is a lot to explain here: (1) why desire is the desire of the Other and (2) why I've rather abruptly introduced the term *jouissance* into the discussion.

In "The Meaning of the Phallus," Lacan's own discussion of the relation of *jouissance*, desire, and demand is deceptively simple: *jouissance* minus demand equals desire of the Other (135). But things aren't that simple. Take *jouissance*: "You have the distinction to be made between the *jouissance*, which consists in signifying straits, but clearly combined with something else which Lacan distinguishes precisely as non-signifiers; that is the object small a" ("A Reading of Some Details in *Television*," Miller 24–25). What is more, *jouissance* itself seems to be something lost—the "pound of flesh" one sacrifices in order to keep from giving up on one's desire (Lacan, *L'éthique de la psychanalyse* 370–71). But the "equation" taken from "The Meaning of the Phallus" would indicate that demand is what *jouissance* loses to become infinitized by

57

desire.[9] That is, demand is instituted by a loss of *jouissance*, for which desire is a metonymy.[10] And the object a? Oh yes, it is the cause of desire, that which is precisely not a signifier. Got that?

Jouissance, the object a, demand, and desire can be explained in terms of Lacan's now famous definition of the signifier, which has been lurking behind my discussion of Lacan thus far: "A signifier represents the subject for another signifier. This signifier will therefore be the signifier for which all the other signifiers represent the subject: that is to say, in the absence of this signifier, all the other signifiers represent nothing, since nothing is represented only for something else" (*Ecrits: A Selection* 316). Understandably, what Lacan has said about human subjects and being is similar to what he says about signifiers: "The subject, in other words, cannot come to being; but being can come to the subject as a question which is precisely the question of its being qua subject." Subjects, after all, are signifiers. What happens to this scheme if we assert, as Jacques-Alain Miller has, that *jouissance* is a translation and combination of signifiers—a heated movement from one word to another ("A Reading of Some Details" 24)?

Being, anchored in *jouissance* as a combination and translation of signifiers, is the no trespassing sign (a demand, an imperative) outside of Citizen Kane's mansion and the subject is its question (desire, an interrogative), its "Rosebud?"—the unknown, repressed, and metonymized knowledge about the being within one's life. The relation between demand and desire introduced by Lacan might be better explained if we looked at "Rosebud" as being both a demand and a question, each demarcating a different relationship to the signifier, "Charles Foster Kane." In the position of the subject for another signifier (that is, on the signifier's deathbed, we become subjects by losing *jouissance* and *jouissance* is a combination of signifiers. Remember?) rests the demand, "Rosebud!" In the position of the signifier from which the subject is constituted rests the question, "Rosebud?" What is more, since both the subject and the place (the signifier) from which he or she appears as such are signifiers, each is a deathbed for a signifier; each is a potential subject. The question of being, in these terms, opens onto death and its many guises in stasis.

The other thing to note here is that not only the subject but the Other (as the set of signifiers from which a subject is constituted as such) is barred, not-whole, not-one.[11] Furthermore, without his lack in the Other, there can be no such thing as desire, since the cause of desire (the object a) is precisely that which is *not* a signifier. Back to separation and neither/nor.

In order to bring this discussion back to what Lacan called separation, we need only state that separation involves the genesis of the object a insofar as the object a is *neither* a subject *nor* the Other. Bruce Fink explains the connection between separation and the object a rather well:

> Whereas alienation forces the speaking subject to make sense, to situate his discourse in the realm of meaning, in the "second" operation [separation] the subject is separated from the register of meaning, from the signifying chain as such; but while he is separated from the Other as language, *he is not separated from the Other as desire*. It is in his attempt to grasp [through a question] what remains essentially undecipherable in the Other's desire that the subject is confronted with the cause of his desire. This cause is, on the one hand, the Other's desire (based on lack) for the subject—and here we see the flipside of Lacan's dictum "le désir de l'homme, c'est le désir de l'Autre," which we can translate here as, for example, "man's desire is for the Other to desire him" and "man desire the Other's desire for him." His desire's cause can here take the form of someone's voice, or of a look someone gives him. But its cause can, on the other hand, originate in that part of the Other's desire which seems to have nothing to do with the subject in question. (Fink 94, emphasis mine)

Thus, the object a marks a subject's relation with the Other insofar as the subject is suspended from within the Other by this non-signifier. And the object a marks the relation of the subject with others insofar as they too are suspended from the Other as a cause of desire for some other. However, this is not to say we're all in "this . . ." together. The subject's relation to the object a is eminently particular and not subject to predictive laws—that is, not subject to laws of continuity or regularity. In fact, the cause of desire involves the breakdown of the signifying chain; discontinuity and not continuity is the essence of Lacan's understanding of causality. Jacques-Alain Miller uses the following diagram to explain the concept ("To Interpret the Cause" 33):

(a signifying chain)   S - S' - S''- S'''- S''''
(cause necessitating the
removal of one link)   S - S' $\mathcal{S}$ - S'''- S''''

It is not by chance that the is also the sign for the subject of alienation where a subject has a place, within a symbolic order. This is the subject dictated by the demands of being—the subject who must endlessly invoke its lack or negative capability in order to create or have meaning. This is Camus's Sisyphus or Nietzsche's Hamlet. Not Lacan's. Style may make the man, for Lacan, but the subject is not its own cause.[12] Rather, as Bruce Fink put it, "the subject is confronted with his [sic] cause of desire."

In separation, in the institution of the object a, the subject is afforded the opportunity to cover over its lack and the lack in the Other, to imagine that there has been no loss of *jouissance* in the constitution of desire. Lacan writes this "possibility" as the "matheme" for fantasy: $\mathcal{S} \diamond$ a, con-joining the two causalities produced by alienation and separation: (1) $\mathcal{S}$—the subject as an imaginary foothold (a lack) in some signifying chain; (2) the subject as a desiring being suspended outside some signifying chain by a (that which stands in for a lack in the Other). The object a, then, reduces the Other to the level of an object, which when brought before (returned to?) the Other takes the form of a question, "Is this what you want?" "Is this what you are?" A voice? A urinary flow? A phallus? A void? A gaze? Faeces?[13] Neither this nor that?

RHETORIC, DEATH, AND THE OBJECT a

Contrast this question of desire, this rendering of the human subject as a potential cause of desire, with *the* question in phenomenology and the reification of the name as a possibility within the effulgence of the Other. Look, for example, at Cocteau's *Orpheus* where the question of death is precisely "Who am I?" The response is "You are my death." Not, mind you, "You are death." The possessive allows for the fact that the realm of death is the mirror in which "Who am I?" is doubled and the one is the death of the other.

Cocteau's mistake, I would say, is the mistake of existentialism, which configures itself in terms of a series of ironies revolving around the sophistic chestnut: "Is nonexistence itself a predicate?" Many have observed this in Camus, particularly in the curious sense of the freedom (which he confuses with having a sense of meaning) and the communion (which he confuses with empathy or identification with others) the narrator of L'Etranger finds while thinking, in prison, of his imminent execution.[14] Lacan, in fact, finds just such an "irony" foundational to any existentialism:

> Existentialism must be judged by the explanations it gives of the subject impasses that have indeed resulted from it; a freedom that is never more authentic than when it is within the walls of a prison; *a demand* for commitment, expressing the importance of a pure consciousness to master any situation, a voyeuristic-sadistic idealization of the sexual relation; a personality that realizes itself only in Hegelian murder. (*Ecrits: A Selection* 6, emphasis mine)

And I would find such "ironies" in many attempts to clarify Lacan's teaching, since "to clarify" means, for a number of people, merely to make sense out of something. Unfortunately, only existentialism and phenomenology seem to make sense to many people. Take, for example, Ronald Schleifer's discussion of Lacan in *Rhetoric and Death*. Schleifer is familiar with Lacan's words and sentences, and he writes and thinks well. But he still would have done better to add a chapter on Sartre to his book *Rhetoric and Death*.[15] It would not have been difficult—just a matter of putting "Sartre" where he places "Lacan." Schleifer writes:

> "The subject is supposed to know," Lacan notes, "simply by virtue of being a subject of desire" (1978:253). Lacan's rhetoric functions on the margins of cognition: the subject supposed to know—parent, analyst, teacher—both possess desire and pro-

61

vokes desire. In the first case, desire—like love, or guilt, or knowledge itself—is a metaphysical cause, a "depth" below the surface. In the second, desire is a function of speech, what de Man calls the "figure" of speech, a rhetorical effect. (191)

Schleifer seems to think that the "subject supposed to know" is a person rather than a logical position. To avoid this confusion, Stuart Schneiderman has translated "le sujet supposé savoir" as "the supposed subject of knowledge." The "subject" Lacan refers to is the analysand's symptom, represented by a sigma or summation sign [Σ] to indicate that, in the psychoanalytic session, the symptom represents the possibility of interpreting/summing/finding a signifier for the infinite, symbolic digression from/of desire (a).

Granted, Lacan has said that for transference to occur there must be a "sujet supposé savoir," and he has also made careful distinctions among the transference relations that pertain in the discourses of analysis, hysteria, the university, and the master. But it does not necessarily follow, then, that teachers, parents, and analysts—these "others"—are in fact "that which it is possible to interpret." Analysts may, in psychoanalytic discourse, "speak" from the position of "sujet supposé savoir." But that does not mean they are themselves the analysands' symptoms. After all, the end of analysis is the production of an analyst, not the dismissal of one. When the analysand embraces his or her symptom, he or she learns to speak from the position of the analyst (as the useless garbagification [poubellication] of the saint-homme).[16]

Now see how the same passage from *Rhetoric and Death* would provide a trenchant examination if it were only about Sartre. Desire for Sartre is a dialectical relationship between the freedom of the subject and the effects of that freedom: the recognition of a corresponding freedom of the other that places demands on the subject ("Why Write," 1063b). In terms of a relationship between the subject and an other, desire could certainly be considered "a function of speech" insofar as desire would mark the relation between the self and the other as the bridge between two desiring subjects. Desire is the desire to know (who we are; what we're worth, etc.) in the eyes of others.

But desire is not a *function of speech* for Lacan. Aligned on the side of metonymy (Remember: desire subtends the symbolic but not as a "metaphysical cause"), *desire is a limit in speech.* Desire by itself is not a relation; it is a limit (of the subject S and of the Other A), and as such it marks the impossibility of a relation (the impossible objectification of the Other in fantasy $S \diamondsuit \underline{a}$). I will address this difference between a function and a limit more specifically a bit later in my discussion of the formulae for metaphor and metonymy that Lacan presents in his "L'instance de la lettre."

BEYOND THE ONOMASTIC

Yet, without delving further in Lacan's critique of existentialism or Schleifer's reading of Lacan as a "phenomenologist," it is clear at this point what a Lacanian rhetoric is NOT: Not a rhetoric of possibility, as we see in Merleau-Ponty and Sartre. Possibility has too much to do with demand. Not even a "Rhetoric of Pedagogy: Jacques Lacan and [the possibility] of a cure of Death" as Schleifer would have it. Possibility has too much to do with (symbolic) death.

A Lacanian rhetoric would need to take into account alienation and separation, possibility and potentiality, demand and desire, both death and life. As you will see in the next section of this essay, I see in this logic of the "both . . . and" and explication of Lacan's statement, "There is no other of the Other."

LACAN'S CHALLENGE TO GENEALOGY

The Function and Limit of Speech

The genealogical move would argue that a predicate is predicated as itself, in essence ignoring the distinction between function and object made in mathematical logics. Remember that in chapter 1, I explained this denial of a logical object in terms of a desire to establish a necessary paternity or genealogy that would cover over the desire of the child and safely metonymize that child and her or his desire as the desire of the father. When Lacan writes of being as that which poses its question in place of the subject, this is not to say Being is at one time both performative and constative, at once a function and an object, as Derrida would have it.[17] Rather, for Lacan, Being and Subject are not synonymous: the subject is a function ($); being is an object. I'm not unaware that this point would require much argument. I, however, will let it remain unexplained for the moment; it does seem precisely this designation of being as an object that would allow Lacan to speak very reasonably about "logical time" ("hontologie") while not speaking of "logical being."

Earlier, I noted, as an analogy for Derrida's theory of identity, his use of one of the paradoxes in Russell's set theory. It is not surprising that Derrida—who would deny there is anything that is not a function (an $, an alienated subject)—should have turned to Russell rather than to Frege for a description of that famous paradox, given that Russell himself must be reminded that there is such a thing as an object.

In a letter responding to Russell, Frege summarizes Russell's paradox as follows: "Your discovery of the contradiction caused me the greatest surprise and, I would almost say, consternation, since it has shaken the basis on which I intended to build an arithmetic. It seems, then, that transforming the generalization of an equality into an equality of courses-of-value [die Umwandlung der Allgemeinheit einer Gleichheit in eine Werthverlaufsgleichheit] is not always permitted" (127). To recognize in the citation Frege's rather subtle revision of Russell's version of the paradox, it is important to note that, for Frege, a function is something incomplete, "unsaturated." In his introduction to the Russell/Frege correspondence, Jean van Heijenoort explains:

> When it is written f(x), x is something extraneous that merely serves to indicate the kind of supplementation that is needed; we might just as well write f(). Consider now two functions that, for the same argument, always have the same values: (x)(f(x) = g(x)). Since f and g, or rather f() and g(), are something incomplete, we cannot simply write f = g. Functions are not objects, and in order to treat them, in some respect, as objects Frege introduces their *Werthverlauf*. The *Werthverlauf* of a function f(x) is denoted by e'f(e) (where e' is a dummy; we can also write a'f(a), . . .). The expression "the function f(x) has the

same *Werthverlauf* as the function g(x)" is taken to mean "for the same argument the function f(x) always has the same value as the function g(x)." This is the "transformation of the generalization of an equality into an equality of courses-of-values." Whereas the function is unsaturated and is not an object, its *Werthverlauf* is "something complete in itself," an object in so far as substitution is concerned. (126)

Using this distinction between an "unsaturated" function and its "saturated" object, Frege revises Russell's paradox as follows: "Incidentally, it seems to me that the expression 'a predicate is predicated of itself' is not exact. A predicate is as a rule a first-level function, and this function requires an object as argument and cannot have itself as argument (subject). Therefore I would prefer to say 'a notion is predicated of its own extension' " (128).

A HINT OF A LACANIAN RHETORIC?

With Frege's distinction between function and argument, I would propose the following hint at a Lacanian rhetoric: (1) A Lacanian rhetoric will not just be interested in relations *among* signifiers (as functions), but relations *with* signifiers (both functions and objects)—relations, not the least of which is saying what a signifier is. In other words, one part of a Lacanian rhetoric will be founded on the distinctions to be made between functions and objects. (2) A Lacanian rhetoric will be founded on a logic of approximations and equivalences rigorously specified, as they are in Frege, not on a haphazard series of equal signs denoting the necessary supersession/supplementation of one function with another. In other words, a Lacanian rhetoric will be a response to the preoccupation with metaphor I observed in existentialism, phenomenology, and Cartesian philosophy; and it will be a response to the preoccupation with metonymy (as a ground for metaphor) I observed in deconstruction. I make these rather hurried references to metaphor and metonymy here not only to hint at their importance in Lacanian thought but also to hint at Lacan's recognition of what is at stake when anyone speaks of metaphor and metonymy or entertains "the question of rhetoric": "Finally, if I am to rouse you to indignation over the fact that after so many centuries of religious hypocrisy and philosophical bravado, nothing has yet been validly articulated as to what links metaphor to the question of being and metonymy to its lack" (*Ecrits: A Selection* 175).

METAPHOR AND METONYMY

Understandably, Lacan's discussion of metaphor and metonymy has drawn a lot of interest. People assume that because metaphor and metonymy are "old favorites" in the "history of ideas," they are good places to begin an investigation of Lacanian thought. I'm not so certain. People seem content to say very much the same thing about Lacan's reading of metaphor and metonymy. And I don't think it is simply because there is only one thing to say. Take, for example, Elizabeth Grosz's discussion of metaphor and metonymy in *A Feminist Introduction to Jacques Lacan*: "Metaphor and Metonymy are differentiated both in terms of linguistic orientations and psychical strategies" (103). Jane Gallop, in 1985, said little more than that:

> Lacoue-Labarthe and Nancy present no further deciphering of this rebus. Thanks to the obviousness of the pun in English, their reading of the + sign corresponds to what was the point of departure for me and my class. For the remainder of this chapter I will present my associations with the various elements in the two algorithms. In the spirit of a Freudian dream-interpretation, I will give not the "meaning" of the algorithms, but the necessarily contradictory and errant process of reading of the following formulas. (120)

Even if one were to grant that Gallop's reading were "in the spirit of Freudian dream-interpretation," what would such a reading be except a repetition of a certain precondition Anthony Wilden has expressed much more succinctly, "The difference between the metonymic structure and the metaphoric structure corresponds to the task of displacement and substitution in psychoanalytic theory" (242)? Benvenuto and Kennedy have said this too: "Lacan linked metaphor and metonymy to Freud's concepts of condensation and displacement, both essential modes of unconscious processes" (120).

I would like to take a different direction in my reading of metaphor and metonymy—seeking to demonstrate a relationship between Lacan's understanding of function and object and his specific delineation of the logical operations of alienation and separation. In this light, metaphor and metonymy will be seen not so much as "laws of the unconscious" but as demonstrations of the status of language as a precondition for the unconscious. And Lacan's contribution to rhetorical studies will appear as a "rhetoric in light of the unconscious," not as a "rhetoric of the unconscious."

I would argue that Lacan's formulae for metaphor and metonymy are precisely, very precisely, situated in Lacan's theorization of the subject. Thus, what Lacan says about the agency of the letter is directly related to a discussion of rhetoric because, through this theorization, Lacan does not avoid the type of infinity (the infinity of desire as metonymy) that philosophy has thrown into the trash can along with rhetoric, nor does it create the "bad infinity" (the infinity of measureless application and symbolic displacement) that accounts for the popularity of deconstruction in the United States. It is no accident, then, that at an early stage in his development of a theory of the subject Lacan should formulate a nonphilosophical question about rhetoric: "Can one really see these mere figures of speech when it is the figures themselves that are the active principle of the rhetoric of the discourse that the analysand in fact utters?" (146).

In fact, I hope to show that Lacan's formulae for metaphor and metonymy make a very precise, yet early, formulation of what Lacan will later render in terms of the vectors of discourse and the topology of the subject: the "timing" of the human subject, which is the specification of the subject's very precise relation, as a signifier, with other signifiers. This inquiry into the timing of the subject and the "L'instance de la lettre" will eventually lead to one of the possible formulations of a Lacanian calculus.

I will first present the two formulae for metonymy and metaphor, which Lacan introduces in "The Instance of the Letter," so that we can determine what segments of the formulae require explication. Such a presentation will also allow the comparison of the two structures in terms of similar and dissimilar segments.

Metaphor: $f(S'/S)S \cong S(+)s$
Metonymy: $f(S \ldots S')S \cong S(-)s$

From a comparison of the two structures, it seems the similarities would be the $f()S \cong S()s$. In other words, the similarity is expressed as an equivalence between two "courses of value": on the left-hand side, the bold-faced supplementation of a function by a signifier; on the right, the imposition of a complete set of signifiers. Using Fregean terminology, one might say that on the left-hand side of both formulae there is a function $[f()]$ and its dummy $[S]$—the signifier $[S]$ representing the necessary supplementation of the unsaturated function. On the right-hand side of the formulae Lacan posits a set of signifiers (a *Werthverlauf*) equivalent to the supplemented function on the lefthand side of the equation. At the onset, at least, Lacan seems to conform to the Fregean model of function/object presented earlier.[18] I will speak more about Lacan's notion of the function a little bit later—after a discussion of what distinguishes one formula from the other: the bar and the plus/minus.

THE BAR

The bar appears to the left of the equivalence sign in the formula for metaphor. This is not surprising; the bar is "the bar of substitution"; and one of the ways Lacan defines metaphor, in its simplest form, is as an effect of substituting one signifier for another (Miller, "To Interpret the Cause" 21; *Ecrits* 258). And that is precisely what S'/S means; one signifier S' is substituted for another signifier S. But there is a curious temporality at work here. S' would appear before S—just as "Elizabeth II" made it necessary for there to be an "Elizabeth I." (That is, we needn't count Elizabeths until there are two of them). The S', one might say, makes it *possible* for us to deduce the existence of S, and S makes it *possible* for there to be an S' to start with. As we observed earlier, possibility has a dual aspect for Lacan; only here we see the twin aspects of possibility in terms of metaphor and metonymy. On the one hand, metaphor lays down metonymy, since it is the introduction of the bar that creates the vertical dimension of the signified along which Lacan places both metaphor and metonymy: "We have shown the effects not only of the elements of the horizontal signifying chain, but also of its vertical dependencies in the signified, divided into two fundamental structures called metonymy and metaphor" ("Agency of the Letter" 164). On the other hand, metonymy functions as a ground for metaphor. Lacan tells us that the bar itself is a signifier, allowing us to read "S'/" as either/or: Either this signifier [/] or that signifier [S']. And S remains in place, as a residue of the set of signifiers (S ... S') verticalized, looped, and quilted in metaphor.

My allusion to the either/or choice of alienation is not accidental. But rather than seeing the forced choice of alienation as "Your money or your life," one might see it as "Your metaphor or your life." Although metonymy is quite precisely what must be repressed, given up on (without a choice) if there is to be such a thing as language, this forced choice would not exist if there were no such thing as language to start with. The One-ness of metaphor is given up to language so that it might be returned (one by one by one . . . in the infinite ciphering of the unconscious as condensation) but with a nonsensical fringe of metonymy (a not-one, a not-S' in the infinite ciphering of the unconscious as displacement).

To use some of the language introduced by the example of "Rosebud?!" above, there must be a loss of *jouissance*, a sacrifice, so that *jouissance* might return as effects in a body of language limited by desire (*neither* this signifier *nor* that signifier). There is, then, a loss in the translation and combination of a set of signifiers (S2) so that the choice of "there being one signifier and one signifier alone" (S1, the choice of being: the signifier of non-meaning) can return in the sphere of meaning (S2) as a loss.[19]

In this manner, metaphor and metonymy represent Lacan's conception of "alienation" and "separation" at their most "abstract" and "literal" level.

THE MINUS AND THE PLUS

Three years before he presented "L'instance de la lettre," Lacan wrote in his *Seminar II*, "Everything comes back to 'to be or not to be [English in the original]' to the choice between what will or won't come out, to the primordial couple of plus or minus" (192). Here Lacan's notion of choice is introduced in a more specific fashion than I presented earlier. I hope to demonstrate that this choice Lacan speaks of is related to what he calls the "instance of the letter" and, eventually in my presentation of a Lacanian calculus, to what I have already identified as the logical operation of "separation" in Lacanian thought.

If this seems a rather grandiose thing to say about pluses and minuses, I might speak, for a moment, of the claims John Grandi made, in 1703, about the relation of pluses and minuses when he observed that $1 - 1 + 1 - 1 + 1 - 1 + 1 \ldots$ from one perspective is $(1 - 1) + (1 - 1) + \ldots = 0$, and from another is $1 + (-1 + 1) + \ldots = 1$. Grandi says God must have used a technique based on this series (now called a "Grandi series") in order to create Something from Nothing (cited in G. H. Hardy, *Divergent Series* 55–59). So that we might not dismiss Grandi out of hand, I would ask if Grandi's claim is so much different from the claims of some modern physicists that the cosmos is a *moire*, an interference pattern produced by a wave function out of phase with itself?[20] My reading of the Grandi series would be to say that what it demonstrates is the function (expressed as parentheses above) of the cut, which is precisely that "without the cut, we don't count" because without the cut the timing of the subject does not begin. As Lacan himself writes, again in *Seminar II*, "the human subject doesn't foment this game [of pluses and minuses], he takes his place in it, and plays the role of the little pluses and minuses" (192).

What I would introduce, at this point, is the possibility that these pluses and minuses are not constituted as a differential series solely but that they operate as directions of force—that is, as vectors which, in the 1970s, Lacan finds formalized very precisely in knot theory.

The reading of pluses and minuses as "directions of force,"

however, does not ignore Lacan's own 1950s explication of the minus and the plus:

1) the sign — placed between ( ) represents here the maintenance of the bar—which in the original algorithm marked the irreducibility in which, in the relation between signifier and signified, the resistance of significative is constituted.
2) the sign + between ( ) represents here the crossing of the bar — and the constitutive value of the crossing for the emergence of signification. *Ecrits: A Selection* (164)

ADDITION, SUBTRACTION, AND THE BAR OF SUBSTITUTION

I have already covered much of this territory in my discussion of "the bar." The plus sign that dances in the void () between the signifier S and the signified s is composed of two bars of substitution (the bar crossed (−) and the bar that crosses (l). In this manner, Lacan indicates that metaphor is the result of the positivization of a negative (the literal positivization of the bar of substitution)—how in metaphor, a "minus" becomes a "plus." I need to be very careful here, though. I do not mean that the minus is somehow changed into a plus or that metonymy is made into metaphor. I say a minus becomes a plus because that does not mean the minus is gone. On the contrary, the minus is present as a metonymy of the plus—a precondition for the plus, a precondition whose absence is felt only as the meaning (signification) of the plus passes through it (as the meaning of Elizabeth II passes through the being of Elizabeth I). Thus, the plus and the minus, on the right-hand side of the formulae, reiterate (are equivalent to, "≅") the relation between metaphor and metonymy that the previous analysis of the bar of substitution uncovered on the left-hand side of the formula for metaphor.

To recognize in the plus and minus the operations of addition and subtraction will take the discussion of metaphor and metonymy a little farther. I would suggest that addition and subtraction represent directions toward zero on a number line. That is, minus represents a direction from the left and plus represents a direction toward the right. Metaphor, in these terms, would be the institution of zero, the crossing of the bar of substitution that allows a number line to continue with 1, 2, 3, 4, 5, and so on, as well as to back track along a path that we might not say is not "really there." Metaphor, in these terms, is the possibility for substitution itself reinscribed, in essence positivized, in the register of -1, -2, -3, and so forth.

That numbers may be described with reference to zero may seem problematical to some, but it is in these terms that Lacan introduces the signified, the little s, into the right side of his formulae. If, for example, addition means summing two numbers, then wouldn't it be a movement to the left of a number: adding two and one means running as fast as one can to the right of the number line, until one slams into a wall marked "three: no trespassing"? What does zero have to do with this summing? Everything, if you see in addition and subtraction, in their coupling with zero, the very essence of a number's identity.

In his 1967 essay, "Suture," Jacques-Alain Miller explains that 0 is a concept that is not identical with itself: $n + 1$. Zero thereby renders lack visible and grounds "truth" in that which is apparently not identical with itself, all at the place where the subject is a structure of repetition (30–31). What Miller expresses here, in part, is the fact that any number takes its place *with reference to* zero and takes its place *as* zero. Frege expresses this identity of a number as a relation to zero by placing a bar over the number: four becomes **4**. Zero introduces the order of cardinality (the order of the signified) into a number system; the fourthness of four or the thirdness of three is an effect of place that zero has given to the number and an effect of the part that zero has taken away from it.[21] Paradoxically, to become the essence of itself, a number must take a loss, must be barred and be a bar (a site of substitution). Any number, in these terms, is itself a plus or minus zero, flitting in a void that separates the signifier from the signified: S()s, where S is signifier and s is signified.[22]

But where is our little *a*, the cause of desire? The little *a* which is produced in separation? Have we come this far only to clothe "alienation" in the nicely tailored pants of some number theory?

Lacan pushes us farther along in his conceptualization of infinity and its relation to desire. To read the − and the + as directions allows us to begin a formalization of an infinity that is beyond philosophical categories of ontology and epistemology and even their inevitable conflation in the onto-epistemology of Western theology.[23] Lacan has not only accepted the infinity Descartes and Derrida throw in the wastebasket along with rhetoric, but he formalizes the logic of this relation of infinity and rhetoric, this logic of the wastebasket if you will, in terms of rhetoric, in terms of metaphor and metonymy. In speaking of metonymy, in particular, Lacan writes: "And the enigmas that desire seems to pose for 'natural' secret collusion with which it envelops the leisure of knowing and of dominating with *jouissance*, these amount to no other derangement of instinct than that of being caught in something else—of metonymy" (*Ecrits: A Selection* 167). In this respect, metaphor and metonymy become formalizations of time and of the human subject in terms of time—not only in terms of anticipation and reflection as Ellie Ragland-Sullivan has brilliantly pointed out ("Counting from 0 to 6"), but in terms of what Lacan calls later in *Seminar XI*, "the mediation of the infinity of the subject with the finiteness of desire" (252). But what does this mean? The infinity of the subject? The finiteness of desire? And what do these two expressions have to do with metaphor and metonymy? And the object a?

INFINITY

To answer that question, let me first establish the relationship between zero and infinity I believe Lacan assumes above. One way to speak of the relation of zero and infinity in mathematical logic is to speak of what the popular mathematician Rudy Ruker has called, after David Hilbert, "Hilbert's Hotel." One of the most curious things about Hilbert's Hotel, which has an infinite number of rooms, is that even after it fills up, more and more people can be squeezed in, without making them bunk together. Say, for instance, that an infinite number of guests have arrived. Now, say that one more guest arrives with letters of introduction from Georg Cantor: Guest Omega. One certainly could not send such a person away. But how shall we find appropriate accommodations for her? We can put Guest Omega in Room 0, which is emptied by moving Guest 0 to Room 1, which is emptied by moving Guest 1 to Room 2, which is emptied by . . . (Rucker 47). What Rucker's explication of Hilbert's Hotel demonstrates is that zero makes a nonactualized infinity possible but in the place of the impossible, which is precisely why Jacques-Alain Miller says that zero is $n + 1$; zero is what makes real the impossible, without the intermediary notion of "the possibility of the impossibility." After all, zero, as I've already explained, makes possible the positive and negative numbers and not vice versa. This is why Lacan can say in the sixties that psychoanalytic praxis is the use of the symbolic to work on the real.

Is it possible, then, to associate infinity and zero with metaphor and metonymy? Lacan seems to make this association when he writes of the infinity of the subject and the finiteness of desire. Desire is related to metonymy as well as to time in Lacan's definition of interpretation from *The Four Fundamental Concepts*: "Interpretation concerns the factor of a special temporal structure that I have tried to define in the term metonymy" (176). I refer to this later text by Lacan because I think it a clearer statement of what Lacan means when he writes in "L'instance de la lettre" that desire mocks the abyss of the infinite catching us in the rails of metonymy. Notice, in that statement, it is the rails of metonymy that eternally stretch forward toward desire. A subject might be caught in those rails and thereby finitized, but that is not to say desire itself is finite. In fact, I would read it to say that Lacan places metonymy on the side of the combinatory infinite that functions as a limit within what Lacan has called, in "Kant with Sade," "the calculus of the subject." Zero, in these terms, would also be a limit but a limit placed on the side of metaphor, since as I said earlier, zero is the mark of having passed from nonsense to sense which allows one to establish the logical priority of negative numbers after having established the logical posteriority of positive numbers.

Further, just as Lacan associates metonymy with desire in this essay, he associates metaphor with what he calls the symptom (Σ) within which "flesh or function is taken as a signifying element" (166). The relation between flesh and function here demonstrates a relation between zero and metaphor that is not addressed directly by Lacan until his study of the topological figure of the torus.[24] By relating function to flesh, in this earlier period of his thought, Lacan is observing that zero is the formal equivalent of a tattoo (m-0-m), the mark of a lack that inscribes a double lack insofar as the presence of the signifier demonstrates the absence of the places from which it signifies. I will speak more about the relation of metaphor and metonymy to the body in chapter 4. The example of Hilbert's hotel has better prepared us for a discussion of Lacan's notion of the function, since with infinity (metonymy) and zero (metaphor) designated as limits or "unassailables," the calculus within which functions may operate is made possible.

THE FUNCTION

I would like to say a word about Lacan's use of the function, f(), in his formulae. In some sense, I've already begun to do so in my previous discussions of Frege and the Grandi series where, in the first, the function was opposed to logical objects/courses of value and, in the second, the function is parsed as cuts within a series of signifiers. Gustav Euler provides a definition of function sufficiently generalized to accommodate both Frege and Grandi: "If some quantities depend on others in such a way as to undergo variation when the latter are varied, then the former are called functions of the latter" (cited in Kline, *Mathematical Thought from Ancient to Modern Times* 506). It is a start, then, to say that a function marks a particular relation among signifiers. But what sort of relation? Contrast function with the type of relation specified by the stroke mark after the S in the formulae presented above, where the stroke is an indication of the possibility of substituting one signifier for another within a context specified by a particular series of signifiers. Logicians call this principle of substitution, after Leibniz, "the principle of substitution *salva veritate*."[25] A function,

I would say, has more to do with Leibniz's notions of incomparability than it does with his notions of substitutability, since Leibniz's notion of the function is a result of his work with infinitesimals or, more precisely, his use of infinitesimals as formalizations of limits within his calculus. I will quote extensively from Leibniz here, since his work hints at the antinomy between metaphysics and infinity discussed earlier in chapter 1 and hinted at by Lacan in an example cited above:

> My intention was to point out that it is unnecessary to make mathematical analysis depend on metaphysical controversies or to make sure that there are lines in nature which are infinitely small in a rigorous sense in comparison with our ordinary lines, or as a result, that there are lines infinitely greater than our ordinary ones. . . . This is why I believed that in order to avoid subtleties and to make my reasoning clear to everyone, it would suffice here to explain the infinite through the incomparable, that is to think of quantities incomparably greater [infinity] or smaller [zero] than ours. ("Letter to the mathematician Varignon [February 1702]" 542–43)

For Leibniz, infinitesimals are incomparables at which something might be directed but which can never be reached. They cannot even be expressed as a relation between two numbers but as the relation of a number to the infinitesimal itself. Infinitesimals structure comparables, which are, in turn, open to substitution. This is not to say that zero and infinity are themselves functions, certainly not, but that a function is an evacuation of meaning in terms of the limits within which substitution is possible.

What is even more surprising is that Leibniz seems to hint at the relation of the infinitesimal and validity that Lacan is able to make in his reading of the Cretan Liar's paradox (*Seminar XI* 46). That is, Leibniz hints at that logic of the impossible, which Lacan will develop in response to the structuralists' dependency on a notion of the metalinguistic in their theory building. Leibniz writes:

> These incomparable magnitudes—are not at all fixed or determined but can be taken to be as small as we wish in our geometrical reasoning and so have the effect of the infinitely small in a

rigorous sense. If any opponent tries to contradict this proposition, it follows from our calculus that the error will be less than any possible assignable error since it is in our power to make the incomparably small magnitude small enough for this purpose inasmuch as we can always take a magnitude as small as we wish. (*Opuscules et fragments* 371)

IMPOSSIBILITY AND THE CALCULUS OF THE HUMAN SUBJECT

I do not doubt that some would see in Leibniz's discussion of error more an early reference to what is called the derivative of a function than some such nonsense as a "logic of the impossible." I know I have not been clear about what a "logic of the impossible" might be. I hope now to show that the instance of the letter is an early formulation of this logic of the impossible insofar as the problem of defining an "instance" (an impossibility) is what calculus was designed to address.

The impossible problem of definition that calculus addresses might be explained in terms of the problem of specifying the speed of a cantaloupe at the very instant it is about to strike a large brown rat. Of course, to calculate the average speed of the cantaloupe, one need only take the distance traveled during some interval of time and divide it by that amount of time. But try applying this concept to the speed of a cantaloupe at an instant. Divide the distance the cantaloupe travels in one instant (0) by the time that elapses during one instant (0), and the result is 0/0. A "meaningless expression?" As meaningless as "the logic of the impossible?" (Kline, *Mathematics for the Nonmathematician* 368). That is, to make meaning of the expression 0/0 is impossible. And any logical system that could do so would be a logic of the impossible—a logic of the instance or instant. I use the phrase "logic of the impossible," but in the phenomenological period of Lacan's career what appears is more a logic of the nonsensical or the paradoxical.[26]

Lacan's investigation of the impossible really marks a movement into his structural period. At this point in my investigation, it would be more appropriate to specify the relation between the means by which a calculus and a Lacanian rhetoric can derive an instant. First, a discussion of calculus—which I've adapted from Morris Kline's *Mathematics for the Nonmathematician*.

For the purpose of illustration, I will recall the problem of the rat and the cantaloupe presented earlier. Only now I will map the trajectory of the melon onto an x/y axis. To determine the instant y of the cantaloupe's trajectory, one need only read the instantaneous rate of change at y with respect to the value of an x designated at x_1. Mathematicians have a name for this instantaneous rate of change of y compared to x at the value x_1 of x; they call it a derivative. For the function $y = x^2$, let's say, a point P might be designated by assigning the arbitrary value 2 (X_1) for x. The coordinates of the point P would then be (2,4). To go farther and determine the derivative of the function and its geometrical equivalent—the slope—one need only then increase the independent variable by some value k and increase the dependent variable by some value h. For the function, $y = x^2$, then, the quantities x + h and y + k could then be interpreted as coordinates of a point on the curve representing the function $y = x^2$; that point might be designated as Q. To approach the value of an instant y then is to calculate the average of k/h as k and h approach zero. That is, as h approaches zero, point Q comes closer to point P and line PQ comes closer and closer to the line touching the trajectory of the cantaloupe at P. In other words, since k/h is the slope of PQ, the instant y in relation to x at x = 2 is the slope of the line that touches the curve at P (with the coordinates 2,4) (*Mathematics for the Nonmathematician* 379–82).

BACK TO METAPHOR AND METONYMY AND A VISIT FROM THE OBJECT a

And Lacan's use of metaphor and metonymy in his determination of the instance of the letter follows the same tertiary movement whereby the movement from one number to the next calls up a zero (metaphor) that creates and is situated in the place of an infinity having no claim on it (metonymy). Thus, when Lacan speaks of the slope of metaphor and metonymy, he is speaking very precisely about a particular relation of signifiers that has as its referent the creation of the human subject as a lacking being—this is to say, the human subject as a timing or instance of the letter. The $ falls out of symbolic order demarcated by the line PQ in the cantaloupe illustration above, grounding the symbolic order infinity (metonymy), "a word for a word for a word for a word; a thought of a thought of a thought," in the metaphorical cut of language that introduces a void into the world through language. This is what it means to say the subject is a function of language, quite literally, a $y = x^2$ for example, which is constituted by a particular relation among signifiers whose identity is only determinable as subject positions for other signifiers. In Fregean terms, the subject as function is unsaturated and its identity must then be as a "dummy" approached within the closed field of its own courses of value; in Grandian terms, the subject as function is the interval between two particular syncopations of pluses and minuses that have as their effect either a one or a zero.

But why call this discussion of the relation of a subject to language a Lacanian rhetoric? Surely, not all language theory or philosophies of language are rhetorics. No, in fact, what Lacan teaches is that no theory or philosophy of language is a rhetoric except inasmuch as it is able to formulate rhetoric as something in the impossible position of a metalanguage: as the P in the series "P of a Q of a Z of a T of a . . ." However, I would not choose to call anything a rhetoric that would have as its aim a dismissal of rhetoric. It may be impossible for rhetoric to exist as a metalanguage, but that is not to say rhetoric cannot insist as a metalanguage, as a timing, or as an instance.

I say the position marked P above is impossible because it introduces an infinity that branches only to the right. If the position P were not, in fact, impossible, it would introduce a structure that would branch to the left as well. But it doesn't. There is no ". . . of an X of a P of a Q of a . . ." Furthermore, even if there were, then one could not say P introduced an infinite series. This impossibility of a metalanguage, of a P, then, materializes a necessary cut in the infinite that is recovered as the truth conditions for establishing P as that which itself introduces an infinite series. The infinite, then, is founded on a cut or a twist in itself. Although I had wanted to limit my discussion to Lacan's phenomenological period, it might be helpful to introduce the Möbius strip as a way to explain the impossibility of a metalanguage. The Möbius strip is twisted in such a way that it is a one-sided three-dimensional object. That is, if a person were to take a pencil and run it along the surface of a Möbius strip, that person would find that the line drawn on the surface would eventually run into itself. A metalanguage, in this respect, is more the recognition that nothing in language is ever thrown away; there is no clean sheet of paper to write on, but a palimpsest from which to work and a message that resists not being (not) written.[27]

To say that rhetoric insists as a metalanguage is misleading; it is the study of how the act of finding is an act of creation. For Lacan, people literally find their ways; they are self-made. In fact, Lacan's discussion of rhetoric in terms of Quintilian's list of "tropes" would support this view, since Lacan says, in the same essay, that the word *trope* is etymologically related to the French *trouver*. A tropology, then, from a Lacanian point of view would be a science of finding based on the assumption that, wherever one may be coming from, there is always something to find—which is, in part, what calculus teaches us in its examination of the instance via functions and derivatives. After all, whether or not a person starts with $X = 2$ or $X = 4791$, the logical relation between an independent and dependent variable is recoverable as one instance of the dependent variable.

"Finding one's way" (finding one's cause), however, is not merely a movement from "fact" to "sense" or from a "given" to its "conditions of possibility." As I will show in chapter 4, "finding one's way" also has much to do with what is lost in one's life; more specifically, it has much to do with the logical and causal formation of loss in terms of time and choice.

4

LACAN, ARISTOTLE, AND
THE SCIENCE OF WRITING

In the first chapter, I proposed an *experimentum mentis* of sorts: If the exclusion of rhetoric as a theoretical discipline is characterized by a choice between it and geometry, then one recourse for the rhetorician—one way for rhetoricians to define the object of their particular inquiries—is to examine the work of those who have not found rhetoric and geometry to be antithetical intellectual pursuits. One of the challenges facing such a project was to establish the truth conditions for statements about philosophy, rhetoric, and geometry solely by investigating the work of a few particular philosophers, rhetoricians, or geometers. In other words, from the standpoint of establishing a verification model for this study, my readings of individual thinkers could not have been simply exemplary, but they must have taken on attributes of the paradigmatic. I understand that to say my analysis "must have taken on attributes of the paradigmatic" will seem presumptuous at this point. And for good reason! I have not yet demonstrated how it might be possible to move beyond a discourse of opinion concerning rhetoric. But if Lacan is placed with Aristotle, if the early "geometricization" of Lacan's rhetoric is seen to work on a problem that Aristotle specifies in his rhetoric as a difficulty in assigning truth value to *now-*

statements, then I believe one may see quite clearly how one action—the introduction of a zero-function into a series of elements—makes the move from the exemplary to the paradigmatic possible.

In fact, one might argue, without any fear of contradiction from me, that what I presented in chapters 2 and 3 was merely a little story about how some ragamuffin of a zero has tried to find its way home: traversing the great desert of the genealogical (which I understand is located just outside of Irvine, California); sailing over the ocean of the onomastic to stop only briefly at a German vacation spot popular with seventeenth-century French philosophers; heading on, then, to Athens but finding there only another place from which to begin its travels anew: Aristotle's god.

Even those who are not offended by my little story may find it out of place. Yet, if as I suggested in chapter 1, rhetoric is concerned with the constitution of discourse as a social link, then rhetoric does deal precisely with the story of zero inasmuch as zero's is the story of a movement from the exemplary to the paradigmatic.

In chapter 3, I argued that zero is what allows us to get from one to two. Let me now relate that earlier discussion to the relation between exemplary and paradigmatic that I'm hinting at here. Zero, it seems to me, has no place in exemplification; exemplification pretends that we can get from one instance of an object to the recognition of two or more objects (a set of objects) without an intermediary zero. According to this way of thinking, one knows what DUCK is because ducks have something in common—their duckness categorized according to how they walk, talk, and so on. Two ducks can simply stand in the place of "one duck" because of the commonality shared between one and two: what is true of one duck because of its duckness is true of any other creature insofar as it is a duck but not any duck in particular. Each duck then must carry the burden of being IT, the duck, the one to which two ducks/three ducks . . . refers. A brief reference to Kant's *Logic* might clarify the process of concept formation I'm trying to delineate above as a series of ones (ducks) being identified with another one (duck). Notice how, in this passage, Kant does away with the function of zero (which could also, but in this context only, be called "the evacuation of the Other"):

In order to make our presentations into concepts, one must thus be able to compare, reflect, and abstract, for these three logical operations of the understanding are the essential and general conditions of generating any concept whatever. For example, I see a fir, a willow, and a linden. In firstly comparing these objects, I notice that they are different from one another in respect of trunk, branches, leaves, and the like; further, however, I reflect only on what they have in common, the trunk, the branches, the leaves themselves, and abstract from their size, shape, and so forth; thus I gain a concept of a tree. (76)

It is not enough to say Kant assumes a certain notion of reference in this passage. Certainly, when he says I *see* "a fir, a willow, and a linden," one can assume he does not mean he sees the "words" for those objects. But how does he account for the particularity of the three? There are three objects, but they are not just any three objects: they are a fir, a willow, and a linden. The objects, one might say, have already been thrown through the door of the Other and have acquired a place there; "Fir," "Willow," and "Linden" are already signifiers. That is, the "objects" themselves must have gone through the process of concept formation Kant describes in order to function as "Fir," "Willow," and "Linden" in his example. They must have each become a "one," a concept of "a Fir, a Willow, and a Linden." Notice too that Kant speaks of, at the end of the process, "*a* concept of *a* tree." And so, it appears that one has over the course of this passage moved from a bunch of "things" to one "concept" (Tree). However, insofar as "Fir, Willow, and Linden" are already concepts (a series of ones, in Kant's scheme), we have not made the move from plurality to singularity. We have moved from a series of ones to another potential member of that series, another "one," *a* concept. And Kant's reliance, later in the text, on such terms as "higher and lower concepts," "ground of cognition," and "partial concept" would support such a reading of the passage insofar as Kant attempts, using this vocabulary, to account for the singularity of one: how one does not necessarily equal one.[1] And the project Kant sets up for himself is difficult. If the process of conception formation leaves us with a "one," as Kant asserts, he is not allowed—within his "system"—to imagine such things as "that's a one-one; that's a one-two; that's a one-three."[2]

Thus, reference (even as anaphoric or cataphoric movements within a particular register) is elided in two respects in Kant's theory of concept formation: (1) what one sees is already caught within the circuit of concept formation, and (2) the result of concept formation is a "one" which, because it cannot be counted but as one, cannot symbolize a distinction between a one-one and another-one.

When I speak of the paradigmatic, I refer to the not-so-simple act of distinguishing between a one-one and another-one—the not-so-simple act of saying, "There exists one X such that . . ." Existence, as Kant found out, is a very difficult thing to prove if one treats the Other as if it were something that only functions insofar as it does not exist, but existence is impossible to "prove" if the Other does exist. That is, if the Other exists, there isn't room for anything else. Commonality, after all, is the basis for any ontology; Aristotle's categories might also serve as an example. The problem that I attribute to the act of establishing a paradigmatic instance is precisely the problem of handling existence without some ontological scheme.

This is the same problem that allows for the efficacy of terrorism. If one were to introduce a particular signifier into a shopping mall or movie theater—"Bomb!" "Fire"—what is the result? The Other disappears with some alacrity, and the object is left shining in the wake. But what kind of object are we talking about here? Certainly it makes no difference whether or not there is a "bomb" or a "fire" other than as a signifier. The result is the same, at least in terms of the Other. So, in some sense, we are not simply talking about a signifier, but rather a signifier that has reference to an object that exi(s)ts within the Other (the set of all signifiers) but is, nevertheless not a signifier. And it is this object that gets us to run through the door of the Other, to get the hell out of here. This existent. This *at least* one.[3] This object a.

Now that I have introduced the problem of specifying truth conditions for the "at least one," let me say a bit more about what I see at work in the construction of rhetorical inquiries around "major figures" (Cicero, Foucault, our students), "periods," and "great ideas." Earlier I said that such inquiries assume some knowledge of what rhetoric is. My point is more that such inquiries assume that rhetoric *exists* and, for that reason, one's task as a rhetorician is to divine the "ontological commitments" that rhetoric has entailed in the past, in the present, and for the future. Well, what's wrong with that? In my discussion of ducks and Immanuel Kant, I have already hinted at how such a scheme elides the possibility of creating a reference or object for rhetorical inquiries. Let me now move my critique a bit further by arguing that such a scheme functions only at the level of demand (the imperative) and not at the level of desire (the interrogative). Of course, one might again ask what's wrong with that.

One might just as well ask what is wrong with Don Giovanni's behavior in Mozart's opera.[4] Don Giovanni assumes that WOMAN exists and he goes out looking for her. Rhetoricians assume that RHETORIC exists and they go out looking for it: in Ancient Greece, in seventeenth-century France, in graduate school, in deconstruction, in speech act theory, in the contemporary language arts classroom, and in their own "rhetorical and linguistic intuitions."

Don Giovanni too has his manservant (his research assistant) Leporello keep a running list of his "conquests" and a catalog of them according to nationality and social strata, among other things. But then, curiously enough, Leporello's categories, glutted, themselves turn into metonymies of WOMAN; his list has (in all senses of the word) women of every social level and age, coupled together as a series of binary oppositions (fat/skinny, blond/brunette) valued according to their use within particular contexts. In the winter, for example, Don Giovanni seduces fat women for their warmth; when he's feeling particularly vulnerable, he seduces a sensitive one for companionship (Žižek, *For They Know Not What They Do* 113). And this latter move is precisely what Don Giovanni is about: that curious twist in a symbolic order where "exchange value" (the list, the signifier, even if that signifier is "use" or "practice") takes precedence over "use value" (women, Don Giovanni's passion) by making "use value" merely a form of "exchange value" (Žižek, *For They Know Not What They Do*, 114).

85

The other point to make about Don Giovanni is that he does not desire. *Il odore di femina*; he smells women. And the women in the opera respond to him as if that were true. No longer the objects of desire, women see that Don Giovanni is in the position of MAN, something that they cannot catch unless (in the name of his OTHER, WOMAN) he allows them to. He walks like MAN, talks like MAN; therefore, he must be MAN. In this manner, Don Giovanni adapts to the fantasies of women, one at a time—all the while being a slave to his Other, as if the Other as such might fantasize (Rabinovich 90–91).[5]

But isn't this process precisely what happens in the academy where knowledge must always arrive DOA for fear that it might otherwise arrive COD? One cannot speak of "Lacan" or "Heidegger" or "phenomenology," let only "rhetoric." There is a classical Lacan, a structuralist Lacan, a Lacan of the seventies and the fifties, a Husserlian phenomenology, a Merleau-Ponteyan so and so, and an Alexius Meinongian some such thing. Of course, I admit one must be precise about these things—Scholarly and Precise: denying that there might possibly be some traumatic kernel (some hint at desire) that insists throughout Lacan ("The Real"), phenomenology ("the existence of nonexistence"), or rhetoric (the "now"). But where does being scholarly and precise get us, if we're not careful? It leaves us in a state of blessed difference: "not-the-Momma"; "not-the-phenomenology-of . . ."; "not-RHETORIC"; "not-WOMAN"; the site of the translation of one signifier for another, one subjective position for another, a place where *jouissance* (One-ness) holds sway. The result is a pacified Other, a pacified rhetoric, that keeps putting off its meeting with the Real (as object a).

SCIENCE AND THE LOGIC OF THE SIGNIFIER

I understand that I've been too playful here. I am actually trying to set the stage for a discussion of the passage from contingency (example) to necessity (paradigm) that I promised at the beginning of this chapter. But the Other (whose desire I've rather uncharitably summarized), which forces us to address it in the manner of "periods," "major figures and ideas," and "distinguished applications," had to be scrutinized first. This Other of alienation, (this "I know what rhetoric is; I just don't know what Heraclitean rhetoric is") is the unbarred Other (forming the eternal grimace of *jouissance*) who has not suffered any loss and who denies the existence of that which is not a signifier.

And therein lies the fundamental paradox of the "logic of the signifier." As Žižek puts it, "from a non-all, non-universal collection, one constitutes a Totality, not by adding something to it, but on the contrary, by subtracting something from it, namely the excessive 'besides,' the exclusion of which opens up the totality of 'all things possible'" (*For They Know Not What They Do* 111).

It isn't difficult to see in Žižek's remark three of our old friends: Possibility, the Beyond, and Mr. Imperative. If we grant him that a signifier has its place in a symbolic order only because of its difference toward other signifiers, then the rest of the argument falls into place. All signifiers lack external support and, for this reason, a set of signifiers becomes Itself only as pure difference ($x = x$ as $y \neq x$), as The Beyond. But this reference for the signifier, the Beyond, is not an "external reality"; it is itself another signifier—a "NO," an imperative against commonality.

This creation of the Beyond has a lot to do with science. One "Far side" cartoon presents an "inside" shot of a group of "natives," one of whom sees a group of rather serious-looking people heading toward the village. The native yells, "Quick, hide the technology. The anthropologists are coming." While television *shows* on "science" and "nature" seem to put us in the position of tourists who— like Actaon—merely "sneak a peek" at some WONDER, we are silenced by the fact that this sublime object is put into place "with an eye to our gaze."[6] We are silenced or be(a)sted by this fact, so we don't say it. You see, the "addressees" themselves do not understand their position in the spectacle. What the cartoon indicates is that a subject fails to notice how the subject creates the Other as the guarantee for his or her own inventions.

I'm not simply saying that perceiver and object perceived are one, as one finds in certain popular accounts of Heisenberg's Uncertainty Principle. I'm evoking Lacan's specification of the Other as symptom, as a guarantee, "a supposed subject of knowledge," that an analysand's contingent "free associations" will ultimately receive meaning. In the psychoanalytic session, the analyst's "passivity" and "neutrality" frustrates the analysand's expectation that the analyst will offer him or her a point of symbolic identification. The Other as symptom, the Other as guarantee, must then be confronted by the analysand in his or her own act of presupposing the Other.

If I must invoke Heisenberg's Uncertainty Principle, I would rather see in it an example of how contingency not only proves the lie of universality but also, paradoxically, serves as its ground. Take, for example, recent reflections on the "law of the excluded middle" ("For every statement p, p or not-p") in light of quantum mechanics. A fundamental logical principle, if there are any, the "law of the excluded middle" meets every criterion for an analytic statement—logical truth, necessary proposition, and so forth. But if we cannot simultaneously determine a particle's momentum and position, then we cannot maintain that an object has or does not have, at a given moment, such and such momentum and position. In this manner, the choice to accept the "law of the excluded middle" as knowledge is materialized. And we, as certain philosophers have recommended, may choose another logic in which it does not figure as logical truth.

However, there are limits (object a̲) to what we can choose— limits consistently exemplified by the redundancy of cartoons, science fiction, and fantasy films: when we can choose or do anything "we want," we don't. The reason for this is demonstrated quite nicely by the example of Heisenberg. We must make the choice (of a new logic, a new way of life, a new name) before we can have knowledge of it. The choice between "a logic which treats the law of excluded middle as a logical truth" and a logic that does not is only evoked when that choice is registered as an image, symbol, or nothing (according) to which one might identify. We know there is such a thing as "a logic which . . ." and it's up to us to make it. I would see in the earlier examinations of Lacan and Aristotle a further elaboration of what I'm hinting at here: the possibility of formalizing disciplinary inquiry according to choice and not simply scientific (causal?) law.

RHETORIC AND THE PHILOSOPHY OF SCIENCE

I would argue that a rhetoric always deals with the question, What is rhetoric? Notice I do not say, What is rhetoric for Roland Barthes? or What is rhetoric for Kenneth Burke? or even What is rhetoric for Aristotle? For Lacan? Indeed, those questions I would see as necessary but not sufficient if one were to think of rhetoric as a type of theoretical investigation. After all, those questions really aren't questions about rhetoric. People who ask, What is rhetoric for Kenneth Burke? know what rhetoric is (even if they can't say what it is) simply because their question puts them in the position of those who know what rhetoric is, but just not what rhetoric is for Kenneth Burke. I would see those who propose examinations of postcolonial rhetoric or feminist rhetoric or Aztec rhetoric or n-teenth-century rhetoric to be all a part of this same grand research project. The irony of such a position, this positioning of rhetoric as a research project (what I called earlier an *experimentum mentis*) without even one crucial experiment (*experimentum crucis*) is that it makes rhetoric like a science—as scientists practice it, if not as they speak it.

Indeed, Lakatos, Feyerabend, Kuhn, and other philosophers of science who have followed their lead, have demonstrated quite convincingly that science itself does not have crucial experiments, only research projects. One of the most striking studies of this kind is Koyré's monograph *A Documentary History of the Problem of Fall from Kepler to Newton*. Surprisingly, the one common feature for all of the crucial experiments Koyré details is that they never were conducted. Galileo, for example, did not drop cannonballs from the Tower of Pisa. Rather, as Koyré describes it, he was able "to free [himself] from the conjoint influence of tradition and common sense, to draw—and to accept—the inevitable consequences of [his] own fundamental concepts" (329). Granted, there may be something of the etymologist's last resort in Koyré's description of Galileo—where any "gaps" in the history of a word are plugged up by an Earl of Sandwich or a Thomas Crapper. But I would think Kuhn is more prone to etymological or genealogical thinking when he argues that a paradigm shift is the assumption of a crucial experiment into a research program where the grounding function of the crucial experiment is established only after the research program has already become predominant. This leaves Kuhn still without an explanation why a particular research program becomes predominant in the first place because he does not understand that meaning "means" only when seen from retroaction.

Koyré does not run into that problem because he treats individuals as a compilation of what they as individuals have thought. And Lakatos treats "paradigm shift" as a problem rather than a solution for the historiography of science:

> Mature science is not a trial-and-error procedure, consisting of isolated hypotheses, plus their confirmations or their refutations. The great achievements, the great "theories," are not isolated hypotheses or discoveries of facts, but research programs. The history of great science is history of research programs and not of trial-and-error, nor of "naive guessing." No single experiment can play a decisive, let alone "crucial role" in tilting the balance between trivial research programs. (212)

If the history of science is a history of research programs, then the difference between the sciences and rhetoric may be that rhetorical study has its crucial experiments, which are precisely what many have denied it. "Rhetoric needs a crucial experiment," these people say, "only then will it have the disciplinary status of a science." Yet, when focused on the question of what rhetoric is (if rhetoricians were to read and think and write from the position where they might ask the question, What is rhetoric?),[7] every experiment, every experience in reading, thinking, and writing would be crucial for and paradigmatic of rhetoric. This is how I explain the curious fact that when Aristotle asks, "What is rhetoric?" ethics, geometry, politics, economics, physics, metaphysics, and dialectic obturate in rhetoric's position.

What I am saying about rhetoric is not, I think, true for many of the "sciences." For example, if one were to ask, What is physics? that is not physics. And if a person were to ask, What is geology? that is not geology. In fact, people who ask such questions are called "philosophers of sciences" not "scientists." But to ask, What is rhetoric? that's a question for the rhetorician. At least, one who asks such a question is not immediately sent to live among philosophers, perhaps not even immediately sent to live among philosophers of psychoanalysis.

Lacan's interest in rhetoric is not surprising, given this relation between the question of rhetoric's scientificity and the question itself of rhetoric. Lacan spent a great deal of time dealing precisely with the question, What is psychoanalysis—a science, yes? Jacques-Alain Miller, in fact, has said it is beneficial to treat psychoanalysis as Lacan did: as if it had a very precarious existence indeed; as if "psychoanalysis will have surrendered in the future"; as if its existence were in [a] question (Miller, "A Reading of Some Details" 27). I would argue, however, that the fragility of psychoanalysis is precisely what allows for its formalization in terms of Lacan's mathemes (his little letters: object a̲, Φ, Ⱥ) situated as they are in the place of that double lack that cuts into both the subject and the Other.[8]

LACAN WITH ARISTOTLE

My point in reading Lacan *with* Aristotle is not that rhetoric should be treated as psychoanalysis or vice versa. Quite the contrary, I would say that reading Lacan with Aristotle demonstrates in what way psychoanalysis is not rhetoric. Rhetoric is science insofar as it has knowledge of what Lacan calls the object a̲.

In Aristotle, this knowledge of the object a̲ is translated into two propositions: (1) rhetoric is a matter of time and (2) rhetoric is a matter of choices. I would then like to conclude this study of Lacan *with* Aristotle and of geometry *with* rhetoric by examining this possible relationship between Lacan's object a̲ and Aristotle's discussion of rhetoric in terms of time and choice.

RHETORIC AND TIME

Why is rhetoric a matter of time? I have two answers: (1) because it is as temporal discontinuities (how the past constitutes the future to enter the present) that radically contingent elements constituting the shock of the Real give rise to the Symbolic order.

91

And (2) because we're all cheaters. I'll use my second answer to explain my first.

That "we're all cheaters," that as speaking subjects human beings have always taken a bit of a head start temporally (even insofar as speaking subjects are always born prematurely) is Aristotle's solution to one of Zeno's paradoxes of motion. People are not quite in sync with *the now*, and for that reason *the now* is at one and the same time what paradoxically gives coherence to the temporal order and what makes it discontinuous. Furthermore, insofar as objects may be said to exist in time, they are not in sync with themselves. Hence, the problems Aristotle sees with assigning truth values to *now* statements; the formalization of *the now* would seem to require something other than an identitarian logic. *The now* needs an audience (a chorus or some canned laughter) to chop it up according to the laws of metaphor and metonymy. It is no accident, then, that the three rhetorics Aristotle describes are distinguished according to three different times, three different audiences, and not according to three different kinds of speakers (even though Oedipus's answer to the Sphinx's question, for example, could easily have supplied a possible tripartite categorization of speakers). A logic of times is a logic of audiences. And, as I tried to demonstrate in chapter 2, such is the logic of the enthymeme, which is, in turn, the object of Aristotle's *Rhetoric*.

For Lacan, a logical timing grounds the relation of the law to its exception. That is, in part, what I meant when earlier I said every rhetorical experience/experiment is a crucial one (that rhetoric is not a research program). François Regnault explains this relation of logical timings to laws and their exceptions in terms of Oedipus who was destined to kill his father. In the myth of Oedipus, Regnault observes that there is a law: Everyone wants to kill his father. And there is an exception to that law: I do not wish to kill my father but I wish to kill this silly man who's blocking my way and I shall (49). Thus, a person's future is dragged into the present by the past; "being comes to question us about its nature" ("Agency of the Letter" 168). This is the instance of the letter, formulated on the axes of metaphor and metonymy, that I discussed in chapter 3: "At one level, one learns that the destiny of a given person is to be in grammatical language as metaphor (the subject as symptom), or outside grammatical meaning as metonymy (the subject as the cause [object a] of its own desire)" (Ragland-Sullivan, "The Poetics of Lack").

I would see the place of rhetoric as precisely this realm of effect and desire outside of grammatical meaning, which one might say has logic at its navel. Rhetoric is "style," one might say after Judith Miller; it is the challenge of writing that which does not stop being written. In this way, rhetoric might be seen as a knowledge of the object a that oscillates unseen in a place of lack, like one of those numbered ping-pong balls made famous by statewide lotteries. When I say knowledge of the object a, I don't mean knowledge as a savoir faire, a know-how. I don't even mean knowledge as a know-what, perhaps not even a know-when, but knowledge as a know-how-not, how not to drop that from which a subject is suspended as desiring. Situated at the lack in the Other and at the lack of the subject, the object a is, for Lacan, a locus of incorporation. (Note too that Aristotle aligned his enthymeme on the side of the body as well.) It is the formal designation of that double lack that accounts for the fact that desire, according to Lacan, is always the desire of the Other. In this discussion of the object a, then, it is possible to see that what I'm proposing here is not rhetoric as psychoanalysis or psychoanalysis as rhetoric.

Quite emphatically, Lacan establishes the distinction between psychoanalysis and what might be termed "knowledge of the object a": "Is knowledge of object a thus the science of psychoanalysis? That is precisely the equation which must be avoided, as object a must be inserted, as we already know, into the division of the subject by which the psychoanalytic field is quite specifically structured" ("Science and Truth" 12). Thus, the object a is the ground for the Symbolic order and that is why metalanguages are impossible for Lacan: desire and desire-cum-interpretation of knowledge have the same structure. The place of rhetorical effects is the place of the earliest representations of desire in their link to the Mother—rhetoric not so much in terms of a rhetoric of the gaze, but rhetoric as a study of what makes a person a rhetorical subject ($). In these terms, Lacan makes reference to rhetoric: "This lack of truth about

93

the truth, necessitating as it does all the traps meta-language—as sham and logic—falls into, is the true place of *Urverdrangung*, i.e. of primal repression which draws toward every other repression—not to mention the other rhetorical effects it necessitates that we can recognize but by means of the subject of science" ("Science and Truth" 16).

Rhetoric is only, in one sense, a lost cause and a knowledge of the effects of the human subject's birth into language. That is, to speak of the (im)possibility of rhetoric in a Lacanian sense is not to make rhetoric a lost cause but a knowledge of the effects of language. Rhetoric is not about language but is in language qua timings.

TIME AS KNOWLEDGE

When I write of "Time as Knowledge," I mean that language is acquired in identifications that structure each person's destiny as a creature of desire or lack of desire and that this structuring of desire underlies all accretion of meaning in language. What is more, this structuring, whose principle referent is loss itself, affixes language to time immutably. In just such a manner, Lacan relates the subjects of identification, desire, and time in his "solution" to the famous "Three Prisoner Problem," which appears in his essay, "Logical Time and Anticipated Certainty."

The "Three Prisoner Problem" is usually presented as follows. Assume that, for whatever reason, certain authorities must set one prisoner free. Perhaps the prison is in Texas. Try as they may, the authorities cannot find "at least one" prisoner to set free, so they decide to test the logical powers of the convicts in order to determine who might be set free.

The director of the prison puts three prisoners in a room together, each with a cowboy hat on his or her head. No prisoner can see, by whatever means, the cowboy hat on his or her head—although each can see the hats of the two others. The prisoners cannot mirror themselves, nor are they allowed to communicate with each other. The puzzle the warden sets before the prisoners is this: "What is the color of your cowboy hat?" The first prisoner to walk out the room with a correct answer and a logical explanation for his conclusion will be set free.

To aid the prisoners in their thinking, the warden tells them that, to start with, he had three white cowboy hats and two black ones. The warden then secretly gives each prisoner a white hat, and he leaves them to determine the solution to the problem. This logical problem immediately thrusts us into the realm of possibility. In the room, there might be (1) three white hats; (2) two whites and a black; (3) one white hat and two black hat. How can one move from these possibilities to an existence or identity claim of some sort? Lacan details the "solution" of this problem in three stages: (1) the instant of the gaze or look; (2) the time for understanding; (3) the moment to conclude.

The Instant of the Gaze

Although the prisoners are able immediately to exclude the possibility of "one white hat and two black hats," they are not yet "subjects" in a Lacanian sense. Because they have not yet passed through the "*either* (a white hat) *or* (a black hat)," they have no signifier for which they might be a subject. The prisoners themselves are signifiers of nonmeaning, unalienated, simply a *possible* death-bed, a *possible* subject, for some signifier (S).

The Time of Understanding

In the time of understanding, each prisoner must respond to a binary choice: (1) the warden has passed out three white hats, and I am a white; (2) the warden has passed out two white hats and one black hat, and I am a black hat. Each prisoner must then try to recognize himself or herself in light of the attributes of some other to which they are privy. In this manner, the prisoners have become alienated, not a "one" unto themselves but a "two" with reference to some other.

The Moment of Concluding

The moment of concluding is concerned with the time of "separation": the neither/nor choice that prompts the excavation of the lack (a zero or empty set) grounding (serving as a logical reduction of) the "choice" of alienation. Here each subject concludes that he or she must be in the same boat as the other. Each subject hesitates with the others, stops and starts on his or her way to the door: each must be confronted with two white hats since, if one of the prisoners saw two black hats, that prisoner would not hesitate in his or her approach toward the exit. They all must be confronted with the impossibility of identification without the Other. This subject must now hurry to beat out the Other subjects who must be coming to the same conclusion.[9] The difficulty of this logical time is this: it is removed from our normal reference to the intentionality of the subject. Instead, we are dealing with the intentionality of the Other.

Robert Samuels emphasizes the rhetorical dimension of this "moment of concluding" when he characterizes it by the statement, "I am an X because I am afraid to be convinced that I am not."[10] Thus, identification with the Other is based on each subject's putting the same lost object (the black hat, the zero, the object $\underline{a}$) in a symbolic-order position. There is thus a conflation of the object $\underline{a}$ (the black hat) and the master signifier (the white hat).

But we are not finished. There is a fourth logical time, which some Lacanians have called "the time of the object $\underline{a}$." I would like to call it, as well, the "time of discourse." But only in this sense: the separation of the $\underline{a}$ and the I that characterizes this "time of the object $\underline{a}$" makes possible Lacan's deduction of the master, university, and hysteric's discourse structures from the analyst's discourse. Let me explain.

Lacan denoted the analyst's discourse as follows:

$$\frac{a}{S2} \xrightarrow{\text{—impossibility}\rightarrow} \frac{\$}{S1}$$

Notice how the S1, the master signifier, is kept from being placed under the object $\underline{a}$'s bar of substitution. This little *a* represents the position of the analyst (his or her desire) and marks the beginning of analysis with the evocation of the Other. After all, the Other is surely vacant, since the object ("Bomb!" "Fire!") is present right off the bat. And since *jouissance* (the transference of one signifier for another in the "free association" of the analysand) is surely present (in spite of the conspicuous absence of the Other) the result of this timing—this quite specific discourse of the analyst—is a dissolution of the dialectic between *jouissance* and the signifier, a dissolution that results in the dissociation of the I (the master signifier) and the a. In this manner, the a appears as a non-relation, an impossibility, between a subject and the Other (a non-relation which Lacan writes as $, the subject of the unconscious).[11]

By equating the position of the analyst with the excluded-included object or black hat, one finds that the end of analysis is centered on an interpretation (S1→S2) of the presence and desire of the analyst (a). But since the analyst is careful to refuse all forms of identification (again, the S1 does not fall under the a's bar of substitution), the question of the end of analysis, then, becomes the question of how one can leave this "prison-house of language" (S1).[12]

For Lacan, "the way in is the way out." The analysand must cross the threshold (Σ) of the Other (*Autre*) to become—grasp its *potential* as—the object of analysis (A→a, an analyst).[13] From this "factitious fact" of the analytical session, Ellie Ragland-Sullivan draws a strong correlation between the timing of discourse and the constitution of knowledge:

> Discourse is not only a social link but a stance taken toward the unconscious. The master says no to it. The academic is half-seduced, uni-vers-cythere. The hysteric *knows* something is lacking and she/he accepts to drown in the pain of some version of a master/slave war. The analyst *knows* that the "way in is the way out," the paths of language, desire and *jouissance* as expressed in the sinthome (Σ), the only mark that writes on the body to say that there is a meaning "beyond" meaning. ("An introduction to Jacques Lacan's Theory of Discourse Structure" unpublished, emphases mine)

There is a lot to unpack from Ragland-Sullivan's statement. I would, however, ask to postpone my discussion of the academic's and hysteric's discourse for the time being. Both will return, as will the discussion of time as knowledge, when I try to demonstrate how choice might be conceived as knowledge. Indeed, I hope it will become apparent how time and choice are not all that unrelated as grounds for an alternative to the master discourse of philosophy.

RHETORIC AND CHOICE

To demonstrate how the question of time and the question of choice are related not only to each other but to rhetoric as well, I would first offer, in contrast, the manner by which they are related in deconstructive philosophy. First of all, deconstruction does not entertain the notion that "we are all cheaters," that "we've somehow got a jump on the gun." On the contrary, Derrida argues that people are always already behind the starting line, waiting for some sign to begin:

> Delay is the philosophical absolute, because the beginning of methodic reflection can only consist in the consciousness of the implication of another previous, possible, and absolute origin in general. Since this alterity of the absolute origin structurally appears in my living Present and since it can appear and be recognized only in the primordiality of something like my Living Present this very fact signifies the authenticity of phenomenological delay and limitation. In the lackluster guise of a technique, the Reduction is only pure thought as that delay, pure thought investigating the sense of itself as delay within philosophy. (*Edmund Husserl's "Origins of Geometry": An Introduction* 152–53)

One might then say deconstruction is a philosophy of "the check is in the mail" where a person is always waiting for repayment. I am not being facetious; Derrida himself introduces the metaphor of the "check" in his essay "Signature, Event, Context." In fact, when deconstructionists argue against those who would charge Derrida with nihilism, they invariably use the fact that one's debts are always in abeyance as proof of Derrida's optimism. It is Derrida's optimism that is at stake when he insists in "Le Facteur de la vérité" that letters never arrive at their destinations. No doubt it would be quite disconcerting for Derrida to think, as I believe Lacan does, that debts (*l'être* as the object of the Lacanian neologism, "hontology") would always arrive at their destination because they, out of sync with themselves, are already there, having started the journey ahead of schedule. Checks, then, written on the account of being would always reach the place of the Other where they must be honored. Remember that "the choice of life," which I presented in chapter 3, is a response to the imperative: "Your money or your life." Thus, from a Lacanian perspective, all the checks written on the account of being are bad—which is to say there is always already an attempt to honor those checks, creating a double lack: the loss of one's money in addition to the lack materialized by the bad check. For this reason, Lacan argues that choices are always made in the Real, that place where *jouissance* evacuates symbolic law leaving as its residual exigency an object a and as its semblant a fundamental fantasy: $\mathcal{S} \diamond \underline{a}$. And insofar as rhetoric deals with this "residual exigency" of an object a, it must also deal with choice.[14]

Aristotle too placed rhetoric, specifically in terms of *ethos*, on the side of a knowledge constituted as such according to the choices people make: "The quality of the choice indicated determines the quality of character depicted and is itself determined by the end pursued" (1417a16–17). On the side of that which is not constituted as a knowledge according to choice, Aristotle places mathematics: "Thus, it is that mathematical discourses depict no character; they have nothing to do with choice, for they represent nobody as pursuing a goal" (1417a19). This is not a contradiction of my argument in chapter 2, where I intimated that by focusing on *pathos* and *logos*, the similarities of rhetoric and geometry would become apparent. Introducing *ethos*, at this point, extends that argument. How so? There is a relation between rhetoric and geometry; only here one sees that what makes geometry useful for rhetoricians is its uselessness—the fact that one cannot use it to depict a character (as individual or as hypostatized historical period) pursuing some goal.

CHOICE AS KNOWLEDGE

A discussion of the constitution of choice will summarize all of the concerns delineated so far. In addition, the subject will allow me to address a question some of my readers may be concerned about: What are we supposed to do with this book? If there is some relation between rhetoric and geometry, between Aristotle and Lacan, what use might we make of this "information"? How does this knowledge allow us to reconstruct the choices we might make as rhetoricians?

I think we must first recognize how choices are made. As Lacan described it in his examination of the "Three Prisoner Problem, "to choose" means walking through the door of the Other and embracing one's symptom, not beating the Other to the door.

When someone decides that "I am a rhetorician (a white hat) because I see two rhetoricians (two white hats) before me," such a decision is grounded in the impossibility of ever finding some lost object of desire (the black hat) that evacuates the Other and submits "The Rhetoric" to the bar of substitution: The Rhetoric.

IMPOSSIBILITY AND THE DISCOURSE OF THE ACADEMY

"The Rhetoric" might not be so easily related in terms of academic discourse. In the academy, people are more often held accountable to the Other ("Such and Such is or is not a welcome contribution to RHETORIC") than held responsible for trying to work out the impossibility of "the desire of the Other." Many rhetoricians, it seems to me, strive to be just like "them," whoever "them" may be (scientists, philosophers, anthropologists), so that RHETORIC might have its own conferences and endowed chairs; its own journals, major universities, and presses; its own wunderkinds and old farts; and its own hoops to jump through.

Academic discourse is not designed to allow for the impossibility of some truth about RHETORIC, merely our impotence at finding it: "The truth may be hard to get at, but we'll get at her, somehow." Yet, is a failed attempt more easily assigned a truth-value than an impossibility (a The, a rhetoric in terms of the unconscious)? If not, why choose to create a social link through the university and not in some other fashion?

I understand that many will think I'm speaking in vague generalities here. Some would like to point out that the discourse of the sociologist is not the discourse of the English professor is not the discourse of the economist. Others might even call me a "Don Juan" who tries to treat the particular as if it were universal. And someone might remind me that genuses and species do not have the same ontological commitments. In short, I seem to open myself to reprimand here because there is no such thing as ACADEMIC DISCOURSE—only academic discourses.

In my own defense, I would like to explain why it is very convenient to think there are only "academic discourses." It is the same convenience that examining the possibility of "Feminist," of "Medieval," of "Peter Elbowinian," of "Lacanian" rhetorics offers: (1) one needn't then prove that the Other doesn't exist; (2) one needn't come to terms with the value of an empty set. I would like to demonstrate how these not-so modern conveniences (possibilities, really) may not be as helpful as one might think.

To do so, let me return to my discussion of Lacan's discourse structures. Using the four mathemes we encountered earlier ($, a, S1, S2), Lacan writes the university discourse as follows:

$$\frac{S2}{S1} \xrightarrow{\quad\quad\quad} \frac{a}{\text{impotence}\leftarrow\$}$$

Notice the university discourse creates a movement from what constitutes the end (S2) of the psychoanalytic discourse to what constitutes its beginning (a). This may account for the interest both Lacan and Freud showed for the *liberales artes*. An S2, a body of knowledge, tries to address a something (a) that is beyond signification. Simply because our emergence in the field of language necessitates a loss of *jouissance* does not mean—so the academic story goes—that a beyond, a *plus de jouir*, cannot be signified. And, in some fashion, the academic is right; academic discourse almost works, Lacan says, when he writes $—impotence→S1. The academic subject ($) proceeds through a logic of "neither this nor that will satisfy the desire of the Other" (a)—neither this nor that will bring back the Other in light of the object. For this reason, the academic goes on to create a master signifier, S1. But how does this happen? Where does the master signifier come from?

The master signifier takes the place of truth, that in the name of which an academic subject might speak and/or desire. One might say that the split-subject allows the academic to count. In place of the barred subject (a one-two) there might be another (a one-one), which serves as a "slippery ground" for the alienated subject of knowledge. I say "slippery ground" because the authority of the S1 comes down to a simple "because S1 says so." The S1 is self-authorizing. For example, how does one know whether $2 + 2 = 4$ is grounded by some "law" of arithmetic, or some "law" of arithmetic is grounded by the fact that $2 + 2 = 4$? Even though this is a question that fascinated Wittgenstein throughout his career, both in the *Tractatus Logico–Philosophicus* and his *Blue Book*, academic discourse doesn't hesitate to provide a place for an answer (S1): there is at least one signifier that is different—a one that is different from the group of ones. Again, we encounter a pas-un (a not[pas]-one, which is as well a first step [un pas]).

But whereas the object a serves as the "at least one," the master signifier serves as the ONE. And, for this reason, the academic discourse, as Lacan conceived of it, falls on the side of proof and not that of truth: it is impossible for the S1 to become ONE with its own knowledge (S2). It is impossible for "one to become two" in academic discourse because the S1 does such a good job of molding (retroactively) the zero (a) into a subject of lack and desire (Ⱥ) that the S1 itself becomes a mark of difference, lack, and desire (S2/S1→a). Many people have complained about the "self-perpetuating element" of academic discourse. But Lacan provides a rigid specification of this self-perpetuating process in his placement of the master-signifer under the S2's bar of substitution: the ONE is always a one-minus (*l'un-en-moins*), hence the placement of the object a in Lacan's schema to remind us of the more (*a*) with/in language that drives us (Ⱥ) toward consistency (S1).

Earlier, I said that in terms of academic discourse one needn't prove that the Other doesn't exist, and one needn't come to terms with the value of an empty set. I would like to go over my explication of Lacan's description of the academic discourse in order to demonstrate how I have addressed these two issues. First of all, what is the impossibility materialized (*moterialized*) in academic discourse? It is the impossibility of establishing an equivalence between a body of knowledge (S2) and the differential signifier (S1) that makes that body of knowledge cohere as such. Secondly, how is this impossibility related to the impossible relation (a) between a human subject and the Other we observed in the fourth logical movement of Lacan's solution to "the three prisoner problem?" It is the same impossibility. In academic discourse, the Other is invoked by the failure to make an equivalence between an S1 and an S2. This failure, in turn, leaves the human subject alienated ($) [from itself via the Other] and desiring some consistency (S1). This mark of consistency, however, can force a retroactive reconfiguration of the object a as a desiring subject ($). Then the S1 itself becomes a mark of difference, lack, and desire (S2/S1→a); it becomes a signifer for the desire of the Other, which, in this light, might as well exist.[15] In fact, as I explained earlier, the precarious "existence" of the Other (because of the absence of zero, the $\emptyset$, the object a) in academic discourse is the very foundation for the difficulties the S1 and the S2 have in establishing some equivalence. The subject's relation with the Other thus appears as an impotence and not as an impossibility in academic discourse.

IMPOSSIBILITY AND THE DISCOURSE OF SCIENCE

Lacan's formalization of scientific discourse

$$\frac{\$ \longrightarrow S1}{a \leftarrow \text{impotence} - S2}$$

I want to stress the meaning of Lacan's use of "impotence" in academic discourse because "impotence" is precisely what academic discourse and the discourse have in common, according to Lacan. Each almost "works." Each almost aligns the registers of truth and substantiation. Notice that Lacan's designation of the discourse of science is the same as his designation for hysterics.[16] I won't go into a strict comparison of the two. Suffice it to say, both hysterics and scientists understand that language is not-all (S1/S2—impotence→a). Nevertheless, each must try to find some proof

103

of BEING in the evocation of the Other (a): the hysteric seeks proof of her or his own being ($\$$); the scientist seeks proof of the truth he or she "knows" ("knows"-cum-"desires knowledge" [a]) *lies* (in all senses of the word) present—yet hidden—in the subject of scientific inquiry ($\$$).

I would like to turn away from Lacan's discourse structures for a moment to see if what Lacan specifies here, particularly in terms of scientific discourse, parallels the work of those more familiar to an American audience. I am particularly eager to demonstrate how the antimony between "proof" and "truth," which I proposed earlier in terms of academic discourse, might work itself out in the discourse of science. Also, the function of evacuation of the Other ($\varnothing$) in this antimony will need to be addressed more specifically.

THE NULL SET AND LEIBNIZ'S POSSIBLE WORLDS CRITERION OF TRUTH

An empty set really throws a monkey wrench into logical systems constructed according to Leibniz's assertion that "logical truth is one that is true in all possible worlds." After all, if one conceives of each possible world as a set, then one possible world must be empty. Then how can one treat as logical truths such statements as "There exists a . . ." or "There exists something that is self-identical"? Certainly, those statements do not hold in all possible worlds; the empty set, the empty world, would be the at-least-one-world within which such statements did not pertain.[17] Being the at-least-one, rather than having as a member of a set the at-least-one, causes problems for the "possible worlds" criterion of truth, since for the earlier statements to be logically true, each possible world must have at least one member, but would be false in the empty world.

There is, however, a more interesting point to be made here, with respect to the relation of substantiation and truth. To account for the empty set, a logic formulated according to the "possible worlds criterion of truth" would not be able to make existence claims. Since science abounds with such claims, it cannot be true that science reduces to logic (proof). Well, then, what does science reduce to? Truth? Being? Reference?

ALMOST THE CONCLUSION: THE OBJECT OF RHETORIC

The distinction between proof and truth described above puts a new shine on our discussion of the enthymeme in chapter 2. Remember that drawn from probable premises, the enthymeme is not demonstrative proof, in the strictest sense. The enthymeme is an incomplete (*ateleis*) proof, but not so according to its form but according to its logical value (Aristotle, *Prior Analytics* ii.29[27].2).

Might placing Lacan *with* Aristotle then indicate that rhetoric functions with reference to truth because of this fact? Might rhetoric have its object in the absence of the Other (in the empty set that accompanies the introduction of a set theory into a logical system)? Perhaps. I will then need to demonstrate that Aristotle responded to the choice Godel's incompleteness theorem presents by introducing a "set theory" into his system of logic.

But can Aristotle's text be "reshaped" in such a fashion? "There is not truth or falsity in all sentences; a prayer is a sentence which is neither true or false. The present investigation [*On Interpretation*] deals with the statement-making sentence. The others we can dismiss, since consideration of them belongs rather to the study of rhetoric or poetry" (17a3–6). Indeed, can Lacan's? Aristotle does, after all, define *dunamis* as a "being qua other." And Lacan denies that the Other exists.[18]

Let me respond to these impasses by placing Aristotle's discussion of the truth value of enthymemes and of the actualization of geometric figures with Lacan's discovery of the object a. First, let's see in what sense an "other" can exist in Aristotle's thinking.

ARISTOTLE'S ENTHYMEME AND THE ACTUALIZATION OF GEOMETRIC FIGURES

In chapter 2, we observed that, for Aristotle, the actualization of geometric figures is a result of an act of division where the process by which the geometer acquires knowledge (division) has the same structure as the objects of knowledge actualized by that division (1356b30–35). Thus, the relation between the potentiality and actuality of geometric figures is one of division: geometric figures are actualized by division and actualized geometric figures can be potentially examined by division. And geometers "speak well," Aristotle asserts, because they can treat universals as if they were solids: neither as specific universals, "a man," nor as as if they were universals in general, that is indivisible. What does this have to do with an enthymeme?

Recall that the two "materials" (*stoixeia*) of an enthymeme are probabilities (*eikota*) and signs (*seimineia*). What is more, probabilities are concerned with establishing a relation between universals and particulars by moving from a universal to a particular. Signs also move from the universal to the particular but from the particular to the universal as well. For this reason and because I discussed "probabilities" in chapter 2, I would for the moment like to focus on "signs."[19]

In *The Prior Analytics*, Aristotle is quite specific about how a sign "works": "A sign is meant to be a demonstrative proposition either necessary or reputable; for anything such that when it is another thing is, or when it has come into being the other has come into being before or after, is a sign of the other's being or having come into being" (71a5–10). The other of a thing exists; sure, but it comes into being only before or after. In some sense, the other is never here, always there, always out of sync. The being of the thing (the non-other) is the instance between the before and after of the other. Existence and truth claims are then realized insofar as the sign takes the place of the missing other and becomes in sync with the thing. As Hintikka puts it, "the way in which the context of a known 'now' statement becomes relevant to the word at the different moments of time by becoming utterable at the moment in question" (47). But this may seem only to explicate the latter portion of Aristotle's statement about signs: "or when it has come into being the other has come into being before or after."

There is another important phrase to deal with: "for anything such that when it is another thing is . . . a sign." When x does not equal x, it can be a sign of x, a y. The existence of a thing as an other is as a sign of the thing. Such a statement allows Aristotle to treat "a man" as if it were a universal and not a particular. "A man" can be predicated of many but itself has no predicate. Granted, to say "a man is blue" is to speak about a universal, but Aristotle says, it is to do so "not universally." "A man" is a set of individual elements sharing certain characteristics.[20] A particular man, Callias, let's say, is not a set; he is unactualized, defined according to the set of actions that Aristotle would call his "potential," his "being qua other." Callias's potential (his other), then, allows us to treat him as if he himself were a set of elements about which we might have knowledge, just as the actualization of geometric figures is evinced by the construction of their potential division.

This is not to say that human beings are geometric figures, according to Aristotle. But both enthymemes (insofar as they rely on "signs") and geometric division necessitate the presence of a third term (*dunamis*) in the construction of truth and existence claims. Callias becomes a third term: neither "a man" (a specific universal) nor an indivisible universal, "Man." He is not the actualization of "a man"; "a man" is already actualized as a "universal." Callias is thus a counterpart to the geometer's treatment of solids: a paradoxical treatment of "the particular" as if it were knowledge; neither x as x, nor x as y (as other), but "x" as a sign of x.[21]

Using Lacan's mathemes, we might say, then, that Aristotle's *dunamis* moves us half the way toward a rhetorical science: $\math$→ S1; Calias→Callias's potential. Aristotle has the ONE down pat. The next step is the construction of an "at least one" (a) from the body of knowledge (S2) organized around this S1, this *dunamis*.

GEOMETRY WITH RHETORIC: ARISTOTLE'S ZERO

I would say that this final obstacle to reading Aristotle and Lacan as I would like can be resolved if we can conceive of a very particular relation between geometry and rhetoric: where geometry is conceived as the place of the object a and rhetoric is our knowledge of it.

From this perspective, the Greeks' "disregard" for zero designates that they were not able to keep separate Lacan's little a and his big A (*Autre*); that is, the Other existed for them as a place for the *a* (the non-signifiable).[22] To have had a word for zero, then, would have been redundant because they did not recognize the underlying metonymies that zero organizes.

But just a smudge of a zero is found in Aristotle's theorization of *dunamis* and in its temporal correlate, *the now*.

What isn't found, in Aristotle, is how zero is a *part* (a metonymy) and not just a place, how it might be an element in a numerical series—and without this double aspect of zero (as part and place), the object a, that more in language than language, cannot be read as clearly as it might.[23] As we've seen in chapters 1 and 3, if the A and the *a* are not given their proper distance, language becomes something that some consciousness has meant it to be; language becomes a psychology—the consciousness of some god, as in Descartes, or the (self-)consciousness of some trope, as in Derrida.[24]

For this very reason (and this point is crucial), when Aristotle explores the possibility of a passive faculty (that is, when he contemplates the nonpsychological aspects of language), Aristotle creates just enough of a distance between the little a and the Big A, between the esoteric and the mundane, that some speck of a rhetoric might squeak through. And I think that little speck of rhetoric may be a start—as a response to the verification of the human subject's birth into language—a start at making rhetoric a science of the Real (A→a).

NOTES
WORKS CITED
INDEX

NOTES

INTRODUCTION

1. I take this description of the painting form Žižek's *The Sublime Object of Ideology*.

1. THE LOST CAUSE OF RHETORIC

1. Bifurcation is a common structure of marginalization. For that reason, bifurcation is often the starting point for the reconstruction of symbolic orders within which the "lost" might be "found." For examples, see Jarratt's use of *nomos/phusis* in *Refiguring the Sophists* and Harding's use of objectivity/subjectivity in *Whose Science?*. For a historical study of the use of bifurcation in philosophical discourse (particularly in terms of dialectic), Kierkegaard's *The Concept of Irony* and "The Balance Between the Esthetic and the Ethical in the Development of the Personality" might serve as introductions.

2. In fact, in an interview published in the *Journal of Advanced Composition*, Derrida says that many would be surprised at how traditional his approach to both philosophy and its pedagogy is.

3. "La thèse centrale du discours métaphysique, c'est toujours de poser que tout trouve son sens dans the Tout; de sorte qu'en fait tout est un. Rien donc n'est vraiment sinon le Tout. L'étant particulier est illusoire, ou plus exactment l'être seul est étant. Nous avons déjà vu, en présentant l'objet de la question philosophique, que la question de l'être conduit à passer outre à l'évidence initiale de l'étant. Mais sans que ce débordement soit définitif. Simplement, si l'être est absolument un, en tout "étant", si tout a une vérité, il n'ya plus rien qui puisse justifier une distinction entre tel et tel "étants." *Et l'on arrive à la formule selon laquelle tout est un*" (Juranville 73, emphasis mine).

4. The a priori status of effect and predicate in deductive logic is nicely explained by Toulmin in *The Uses of Argument*. A reference

to the "Aristotle is a Man" chestnut might also be helpful in understanding my point, since the middle term of the syllogism, Man/Men, functions as such only because what is predicated as man in the minor premise can itself take a predicate, mortal, in the major premise.

5. Or, rather, a theorization marked structurally by the predominance of the metaphoric does not provide a formalization of rhetoric because rhetoric is not wholly subsumed under the metaphoric (that is, rhetoric has something to do with metonymy as well).

6. I am addressing here what has commonly been called the "Deductive-Subsumption Theory of Explanation." Karl Popper's *The Logic of Scientific Discovery* provides an example:

> Someone asks, "Why did thread t break?". A plausible answer is that a heavy weight was suspended from it. Now on the classical account, there is an appropriate generalization of law "covering" these events perhaps in the following way: Whenever a heavy weight is suspended from a thread, it will break. Given this (presumed) law and the fact that a heavy weight is suspended from thread t, it follows that thread t breaks. In terms of the law and the fact, the thread's breaking has been explained. (59ff)

Popper then goes on to delineate the structure of this explanation in five parts.

7. My reasons for saying this will be made more apparent in chapter 3.

8. "First there is nothing at all then there is something—the idea of forming a set. The empty set is variously called (), phi, 0. The empty set is something, but inside it is nothing" Rucker (211). For a more formal discussion, see the work of Giuseppe Peano, for example, "From *Arithmeticas principia* (1889): Set of Axioms For Integers."

9. Armand Zaloszyc makes this point as well: "Dire: je pense donc je suis est précisément l'inconnue qu'il s'agit de produire au jour de l'évidence d'un signifié enfin certain et fondateur ce qui est la rétroaction significative, à partir de l'existence de l'Autre, du signifiant je pense" (Baas and Zaloszyc, *Descartes et les fondements de la psychanalyse* 11).

10. *The Oxford Classical Dictionary* provides the following information about Pappus of Alexandria: "a distinguished mathematician, wrote commentaries on Euclid's *Elements* and *Data*, Ptolemy's *Planisphaeria*, and Diodorus' *Analemma*. Pappus' work is primarily of importance for the historical data it contains, but he supplies many

lemmas, etc, to the treatises elucidated, and significant additions of his own, e.g. and extensions of Euclid 1.47 (Pythagoras' Theorem) to any triangle, proof of the constance of anharmonic ratios, measurement of the superficial area banded by a spiral on a sphere, an anticipation of Guildin's theorem, and 'Pappus' Problem' which was taken up by Descartes."

11. I'm suggesting here that the economies represented by "gift" and "study" are different. A gift economy is numbered one by one by one, where production is specified by the presence of the object of exchange. A "study" economy, like a money-based economy, is numbered one by two by three . . . where production is specified by the absence of the object of exchange making, and spending is a means of creating wealth. For further discussion, see chapter seven of Lewis Hyde's *The Gift: Imagination and the Erotic Life of Property.*

12. Although she may not act on it as Derrida does, Kristeva provides a nice constative example of this aspect of the genealogical: "If I know that my desire can make me delirious in my interpretive constructions, my return to this delirium allows me to dissolve its meaning which I suppose to be one and one only but which I can only indefinitely approach. There is meaning, and I am supposed to know it to the extent that it escapes me. . . . This perception prevents the closure of our interpretation as a self-sufficient totality." ("Psychoanalysis and the Polis" 310, 314).

13. Aristotle includes "chance" among the seven causes listed in *The Rhetoric.* And Lacan uses the Greek word for chance, *tuxei,* to signify the relation of the human subject to a particular traumatic encounter.

14. In chapter 2, I will address the relation of rhetoric and logical formations of the body in my discussion of the enthymeme as a *soma pisteos,* a body of persuasion. "Spirit and Bone" is a surreptitious reference to Hegel who, as Slavoj Žižek indicates, recognized "the possibility of 'making a system' out of the very series of failed totalizations, to enchain them in a rational way, to discern the strange 'logic' that regulates the process by means of which the breakdown of a totalization itself begets another totalization" (Žižek, *For They Know Not What They Do* 99). Elsewhere in this chapter I have called this Hegelian logic the "logic of the trash can." At any rate, these are the sorts of questions (of body? of spirit? of bone? of action?) with which "the relation of rhetoric and geometry?" will be seen to keep company in the rest of the book.

15. But to describe rhetoric as a form of interdisciplinary inquiry may also be something of a disservice. That is, if one pays attention to a warning given by Stanley Fish: "In short, if we take seriously the epistemology argument [rhetoric treated as the cause of everything; rhetoric as "the structures that organize how we know"] in the context of which the gospel of interdisciplinary study is so often preached, we will come to the conclusion that being interdisciplinary—breaking out of the prison houses of our various specialties to the open range first of a general human knowledge and then of the employment of that knowledge in the great struggles of social and political life—is not a possible human achievement. Being interdisciplinary is more than hard to do; it is impossible to do" (Fish 18–19).

16. I encountered an interesting twist on this perspective during a rather heated faculty meeting concerning a reorganization of a department's masters program: "Why do we have to test our rhetoric people over rhetoric? We already do, don't we? The skills used in successfully passing the literature exam are the same skills our students will use to be good rhetoricians."

17. I avoid mentioning another rather obvious sense of the word *ellipsis,* since ellipsis as truncation and ellipsis as geometric function are not dissimilar for Derrida: "An ellipsis both of meaning and of form: neither full speech nor a perfect circle. More and less, neither more nor less" (*Margins of Philosophy* 173).

18. See, in particular, Ulmer's discussion of Derrida's "The Law of Genre" in his *Applied Grammatology.* For a further application of the concept of invagination, see Ulmer's attempts at writing a "mystory" in his more recent *Teletheory: Grammatology in The Age of Video.*

19. In an interview published in *Splash,* Vito Acconci expresses quite clearly this "desire" (more of a demand really) to break from the page:

> Interviewers: Why did you initially make the decision to leave writing?
>
> Acconci: Because towards the end of the time I was writing, I started to be more and more committed to the idea of a page as a space to move over. I became obsessed with things like, how do you go from left margin to right margin? How do you go from one page to the next? I was really using the page as a space for me, as writer, to travel over. And in turn, a space for you, as reader, to travel over. Gradually it occurred to me that if I

was so interested in moving over a space, why was I limiting myself to an 8½ × 11″ piece of paper? Why didn't I walk on the floor? It seems like a lot of my first pieces were a way to get off the page, out of a closed room, and throw myself outside into the world" (qtd. in Ulmer, "Handbook for a Theory Hobby" 420).

20. In his introduction to Derrida's *Acts of Literature,* Derek Attridge writes: "In view of a frequent misunderstanding, it may be worth stressing that for Derrida the 'literariness' of text conventionally classed as non-literature is not a matter of their employment of metaphor or rhetoric . . . and he frequently includes rhetoric—the study and classification of purely formal features of discourse—within the domain of philosophy" (7).

21. See Jacques-Alain Miller's short lexicon of Lacanian terms in *The Four Fundamental Concepts of Psychoanalysis* for glosses of "symbolic" and "real."

22. Euclid, for example, chose to put the "operational verbs" of his demonstrations in the perfect passive imperative. David Lachterman explains, "Bisecting a line-segment at a point is expressed as 'let it have been cut in two' (*temestho . . . dicha*); describing a square on a line is 'let it have been described on AB'; that A is to B as C is to D is prefaced by 'let it have come about that' (*gegoneto*)" (65). The significance ("significance" both in the sense of its importance and its meaning) of this stylistic trait for Euclid has also been noted by Lachterman: "First, Euclid does not give instructions or permission to a reader to carry out a specified operation but casts the operation into impersonal, passive form; second, the perfect tense tells us that the relevant operation has already been executed prior to the reader's encounter with the unfolding proof (of a theorem or of a problem; the use of the perfect is uniform in these two classes of propositions)" (65).

23. For now, let the following, taken from Daintith and Nelson's *Dictionary of Mathematics*, serve as definitions of a vector: (1) "An entity in Euclidean space that has both magnitude and direction. A vector can be represented geometrically by a directed segment of a line" (335). And (2) "More generally, vectors can be regarded as mathematical objects that can be added and can be multiplied by numbers (say), but cannot necessarily be multiplied together to give other vectors. In this sense, a vector is an element of vector space"

(336). The significance of the vector from a Lacanian perspective may be, quite simply, that it (along with the creation of quaternions and Grassmann's hypernumbers) makes a Lacanian algebra—as opposed to "an algebra"—possible, insofar as its introduction opened up, as Morris Kline puts it, "a new vista for mathematics—there is not just the one algebra of real and complex numbers but many and diverse algebras" (791). See pp. 313 and 315 of *Ecrits* for reproductions of the "Che Vuoi?" graph.

2. ARISTOTLE'S IMPERATIVE FOR RHETORIC

1. I choose to speak about these two critics, then, not because of their "impact on the field," but because, at first blush, they appear to be quite different in their approaches. As you will see, I don't find Covino and Kennedy to be all that different. Each will try to speak of "the object of rhetoric" as if it were some psychological entity that Aristotle would not have considered a "thing." This is not to say there are no differences between Kennedy's and Covino's work. Their methods are different: Kennedy's is a rough equivalent of what I call the onomastic in chapters 1 and 2; Covino's, of the genealogical.

2. Aristotle, here as well, demonstrates that *dunamis* cannot be translated as "becoming," since the loss of "becoming" is an effect of the failure to conceive of potentiality or potency.

3. This is the stopping point for those who would make of Aristotle an ordinary language philosopher.

4. I find Aristotle's argument to be a much more radical statement about language than Covino's. Covino's assertion of the inherent ambiguity of language still assumes that "rhetoric" is a formal response to the "need" or "desire" to communicate with some other. Aristotle conceives of rhetoric as a response to the failure of communication, the failure of teaching. Rhetoric is not a communicative register with an other or some others, but the negotiation of life into the Other as a set of signifiers, that is, the Other as the set of all that might be said to exist. I will address this particular reading of Aristotle more directly in the second section of the chapter.

5. I choose to cite Tita French-Baumlin and James Baumlin's article precisely because they are not specialists in classical rhetoric. My interest here is not so much to criticize the Baumlin and French-Baumlin article. I simply wish to demonstrate that what I say is a

commonplace notion about Aristotle's rhetoric is, in fact, commonplace—so commonplace that people treat it as general knowledge.

6. For further discussion, see Hintikka's *Time and Necessity*, p. 34.

7. The most comprehensive examination of the logical/rhetorical structure of *Carpe Diem* poetry I've read is Kathy Smith's unpublished dissertation, "Making Much of Time."

8. Lachterman admirably develops this point in chapter 2 of his *The Ethics of Geometry*.

9. In fact, as you will see in chapter 4, helping Aristotle's imperative (S1) and Lacan's question (*a*) to keep their distance is precisely the function of discourse.

3. LACAN AND THE QUESTION OF RHETORIC

1. In his *The Sublime Object of Ideology*, Slavoj Žižek clearly explains Lacan's formation of the graph of desire.

2. Jacques-Alain Miller has spoken of three stages in Lacan's development: the phenomenological/existential (*Ecrits*; 1950's–60's), the structural (*Seminar XX, Encore*; early 1970's), and the topological (mid-70's–1981).

3. Presence and absence in discourse (Husserl); presence and absence within a perceptual field (Merleau-Ponty); presence and absence in being (Heidegger).

4. See Sartre's "Why Write?" 1066a: "The world is my task, that is, the essential and freely accepted function of my freedom is to make that unique and absolute object which is the universe come into being in an unconditioned movement. . . . In aesthetic joy the positional consciousness is an image-making consciousness of the world in its totality both as being and having to be, both as totally ours and totally foreign, and the more ours as it is the more foreign. The nonpositional consciousness really envelops the harmonious totality of human freedoms insofar as it makes the object of a universal confidence and exigency."

5. The relation of the void and impossibility was introduced briefly at the end of chapter two. Aristotle, of course, argued that a "void" was impossible since it could manifest itself only as a temporal discontinuity. That is, if two people happen to moving from point A to point B together and Person X happens to walk across a void and

117

Person Y doesn't, Person X will appear to jump ahead of Person Y. After all, it takes no time at all to cross over nothing.

6. One might say, almost as a joke, that for Descartes's God is knowledge, and for Merleau-Ponty knowledge is God.

7. This is about as far as Merleau-Ponty can get in his discussion—trapping the human subject in the vel of alienation [the either/ or imaginary choices of the imaginary order].

8. See Lacan, *Four Fundamental Concepts*, p. 156.

9. "Demand addresses the Other seeking to convey the pressure of Desire; demand is the conscious link to repressed or unconscious Desire. Desire, as a mechanism of longing, is absolute and infinite, but demand aims toward something specific, some substitute object, and is therefore finite" (Ragland-Sullivan, *Jacques Lacan and the Philosophy of Psychoanalysis* 86).

10. Lacan will even state as much in Seminar XI: "Desire is a metonymy": "Interpretation concerns the factor of a special temporal structure that I have tried to define in the term metonymy. As it draws to its end, interpretation is directed towards desire, with which, in a certain sense, it is identical. Desire, in fact, is interpretation itself" (176).

11. Although I don't wish to pursue the point, I must say that the fact of the barred-Other allows for what Lacan calls a jouissance of meaning, since the loss of jouissance results in the formation of a "not-one."

12. See Judith Miller's article in *Lacan and the Subject of Language*, "Style Is The Man Himself."

13. In Seminar XI, Lacan provides a list of object a.

14. Remember that, for Lacan, the subject cannot come to the place of being, which is *in place of* the subject. Hamlet said it in another way, of course, "to be or not to be / that is the question." This is to say: "either to be or not to be, and neither to be nor not to be," since a moment in the void of "to be" makes possible this question. In this manner, Lacan avoids the existentialist credo. That is, he recognizes the existentialist's *cogito*. He understands that "existence precedes essence" is no more radical a statement than "essence precedes existence," since being does not pose its question to the subject.

15. I should say, too, that I enjoyed reading Schleifer's *Rhetoric and Death*. It is certainly recommended reading, particularly his chapter on Jakobson.

16. "Poubellication" (garbage and publication) is a neologism

which Lacan uses to describe the possibility of understanding his "teaching which has been addressed to psychoanalysts for 48 years."

17. I would see this conflation not merely as imprecision but another example of what might be said to be Derrida's insistence on the ironic "structure" (merely distance really) of "it-ness," "The deconstruction I am invoking only invents or affirms, lets the other come insofar as, in the performative, it is not only performative but also continues to unsettle the conditions of the performative and of whatever distinguished it comfortably from the constative" ("Inventions of the Other" 61).

18. The Fregean elements of Lacan's teaching precede what Roudinesco has termed Jacques-Alain Miller's rectification of Lacan by way of Frege (402).

19. Jacques-Alain Miller makes this point in his unpublished course, "Orientation lacanienne" (1984–85): " 'The first choice [S1] is, in a certain sense, already ruled out when one begins an analysis.' It represents what Lacan calls 'petrification' and 'supports the somewhat confused idea of autism . . . [which implies] petrification through the signifier of non-meaning. The therapist's whole effort, in such cases, consists in trying to bring about an alienation' " (qtd. in Fink).

20. For further discussion of this point, see Rucker, *The Science and Philosophy of the Infinite*, chapter 4.

21. For further discussion, see Dantzig's *Number: The Language of Science* (8–9, passim).

22. My use of the term, *void*, may be problematical. By "void," I mean here the gaps left in the wake of the mathematical function's "de-saturation" of the object: "The denotation of a complete name is an object; that of an incomplete name is a function. . . . An incomplete name was provisionally understood as the result of removing one or more complete names from a complex complete name (as provisionally understood), a procedure that left gaps which we marked by open parentheses. In place of these gaps let us now use Frege's lower case Greek consonants 'ξ' and 'ζ', thus writing instead of '()2' and 'the shirt of ()'. . . (Furth, xxv–vi).

23. In fact, Lacan has defined desire both in terms of a minus (*jouissance* − demand = desire) and as a plus: "In 'Desire and the Interpretation of Desire in Hamlet' Lacan 'quantified' the Desire in common discourse as 'the sum and module of the meanings acquired by the subject in human discourse: Your thing is performed by the

Other in speech.' " (Ragland-Sullivan, *The Philosophy of Psychoanalysis* 82).

24. See Granon-Lafont's discussion of the torus. Lacan's discussion of the torus and the sinthome in Seminar XXIII has not yet been published, even in French.

25. *"Eadem sunt, quorum unum alteri substitui potest salva veritate"* (*Opuscules et fragments inedits de Leibniz*, p. 25).

26. For a contrasting view, see Merleau-Ponty's *Sense and Nonsense*, which attempts to develop an "ontology of sense" by treating "existence" as "the very process whereby the hitherto meaningless takes on meaning" (xiii; xvi).

27. For further discussion of the physical properties of a moebius strip, see Granon-Lafont's *La topologie ordinaire de Jacques Lacan*.

4. LACAN, ARISTOTLE, AND THE SCIENCE OF WRITING

1. The Kantian structure of some poststructuralist understandings of zero provides, then, another specification of the onomastic and genealogical moves of philosophy: both try to treat zero as if it were one. "It is [the] double aspect of zero, as a sign inside the number system and as a meta-sign, a sign about signs outside it, that has allowed zero to serve as the site of an ambiguity between empty character. . .and a character for emptiness" (Rotman 13). Notice the chiatic structure of the last phrase.

2. Kant's project is no less than to offer a philosophical alternative to Aristotle's specification of Being as $n-1$ and Non-Being as $n+1$.

3. I stress the "at least" so that it is clear I am not speaking of some *einziger zug*, here.

4. For further discussion of *Don Giovanni*, see Slavoj Žižek's *For They Know Not What They Do* and Rabinovich's excellent treatment, "Don Juan as Slave." Lacan's own statements concerning *Don Giovanni* can be found in *Seminar XX*, p. 15.

5. In an essay on the film *Thelma and Louise*, I have called this structure, "the logic of wo/man twice lost." It might be interesting for the reader to see my fanciful treatment of *Don Giovanni* literalized as a discussion of rhetoric in Elbow's "believing and doubting game" (*Embracing Contraries* 255–57). Notice in particular what Shakespeare play Elbow uses to describe the various stages of the b.d.g.

6. This paragraph is a paraphrase of Žižek's discussion of the point in *For They Know Not What They Do*.

7. That is if RHETORICIANS might speak not as S-laves to RHETORIC (or as MAN to WOMAN) but as $.

8. As François Regnault has pointed out in his essay "Lacan and Experience," whereas the Freudian method seems to go forward from the singular to the universal, Lacan's method consists in keeping a level of universality, which is an equation, or what he calls a matheme (54). Jacques-Alain Miller has said something quite similar about Lacan's use of *sententiae* ("desire is the desire of the Other" "the unconscious is structured like a language") as a means to keep the Other from telling Lacan what of Lacan the Other should like to remember (Miller, "Extimité," 67).

9. Lacan says that the "anticipation of certitude" is the fundamental form of collective logic.

10. Here, Fink expresses quite nicely what I tried to say in chapter two, "Thank God for Elizabeth II, without her there would be no Elizabeth I."

11. Samuels explains as follows:

Lacan speaks of this introduction of the a as an overdetermination of the symbolic function. He indicates that the fourth time relates to the first time and tries to account for what is excluded by the second and third times. "One can demonstrate that to fix the first and fourth terms of a series, there will always be a letter, whose possibility will be excluded by two intermediary terms" (49). Lacan continues by calling this excluded letter, the caput mortuum of the signifier. That is to say an unusable residue whose contour is continually repeated. Lacan attaches this structure to the object of the drive, because it represents the impossible relation between the Real subject of jouissance (the first logical time) and the Symbolic Other of civilization (the third logical time). This non-relation between the subject and the Other is most often hidden by the second time of Imaginary understanding. (112)

12. S1 is used to represent the possibility of "language" because, for Lacan, language itself is a master discourse.

13. Lacan asks, "What is it that an analysis creates but an analyst?"

14. Derrideans, on the other hand, hope that by proposing some notion of an absolute philosophical delay they will not have to make choices. John P. Leavey, the English language translator of *Glas*, will even say as much with great excitement, "Choices need not be made here [in the place of deconstruction], in fact, cannot be made!" (7). Furthermore, in *Of Grammatology* Derrida himself argues that to pose the problem [of being] in terms of choice, to oblige or to believe oneself obliged to answer it by a yes or no, to conceive of appurtenance as an allegiance or nonappurtenance as plain speaking, is to confuse very different levels, paths, and styles. In the deconstruction of the arche [the proto-], one does not make a choice. That is why a thought of the trace can no more break with a transcendental phenomenology than be reduced to it (62).

15. Lacan also stresses this aspect of the university discourse when he speaks of the university as uni-vers-cythere, meaning the academy seduces by knowledge.

16. For a further discussion of this point, see Lacan's *Television*, p. 19.

17. In recent years, logicians have constructed logical systems, all of whose theorems hold in all possible worlds including the empty one.

18. In seminar XX, Lacan says that for Aristotle there is a "jouissance of being."

19. I would even go so far as to say probabilities are signs. Of course, Aristotle says the two are not identical but that does not mean that "probabilities" are not a subgrouping under "signs." After all, brahma and cow are not identical either. This is not to say my contention is unproblematic as a reading of Aristotle. But notice the trouble Aristotle has when he refuses to admit to this relation between probabilities and signs: "Necessary signs are called tekmeria; those which are not necessary have no distinguishing name" (1357a5). Of course they don't! "Signs that are not necessary" are "probable signs," probabilities.

20. "I call universal that which is by its nature predicated of a number of things and particular that which is not; man, for example, is a universal. Callias is not."

21. This "knowledge of the particular," however, is not separable from knowledge; that is, it does not have a place within knowledge. It is, one might say, a part of knowledge, always having a potential place if only it were separable from knowledge. Notice too how "poten-

tiality" allows us to talk about many things as if we could have knowledge of them, as if they were a set, something actualized, not unlimited: infinity, the void.

22. This is no surprise. Lacan represents philosophical discourse as a master discourse, which ends where the discourse of science begins ($\leftarrow$a):

$$\underline{S1}\text{—impossibility}\rightarrow\underline{S2}$$
$$\$\longleftarrow\text{——————} \underline{a}$$

The S1—impossibility→S2 represents that, for the philosopher, the Other (conceived here as the "power" of language itself [S1→S2]) seems to exist and, what is more, such a thing is "impossible."

23. See Jacques-Alain Miller's discussion of Peano's number theory in his unpublished course, *Extimité*. I might comment briefly as well on the relation of an empty set (here rendered loosely as "zero") to the possibility of making existence claims. If one contends that truth is wholly conventional (simply a matter of manipulated floating on the endless undulations of a circuit of language [S1→S2]), how could that person deal with an empty set? Suppose that no sets exist at all (fusing proof and truth, according to Godel's scheme). In that case, the statement, "at least one empty set exists," would be incorrect. Right? Then, one must admit that the truth-value of (at least) one statement is related to the existence of an object; its truth or falsity is not a product of words alone.

24. These are the onomastic and genealogical moves philosophy which I addressed directly in chapters one and two.

WORKS CITED

Aristotle. *The "Art" of Rhetoric*. Trans. John Freese. Loeb Classical Library. Cambridge, MA: Harvard UP, 1982.

―――. *The Complete Works*. Rev. Oxford Translation. Ed. Jonathan Barnes. 2 vols. Princeton: Princeton UP, 1984.

Baas, Bernard, and Armand Zaloszyc. *Descartes et les fondements de la psychanalyse*. Paris: Navarin, 1990.

Baumlin, James, and Tita French-Baumlin. "Belletrism, Cultural Literacy and the Dialectic of Critical Response." *Freshman English News* 5 (1986): 1–8.

Benvenuto, Bice, and Roger Kennedy. *The Works of Jacques Lacan: An Introduction*. New York: St. Martin's, 1986.

Bitzer, Lloyd. "A New Reading of the Enthymeme." *Quarterly Journal of Speech* 45 (Dec. 1959): 399–408.

Bizzell, Patricia, and Bruce Herzberg, eds. *The Rhetorical Tradition: Readings from Classical Times to the Present*. Boston: Bedford, 1990.

Covino, William. *The Art of Wondering: A Revisionist Return to the History of Rhetoric*. Portsmouth, NH: Boynton/Cook, 1988.

Daintith, John, and R. D. Nelson, eds. *Dictionary of Mathematics*. London: Penguin, 1989.

Dantzig, Tobias. *Number: The Language of Science*. New York: Macmillan, 1954.

Derrida, Jacques. *Acts of Literature*. Ed. Derek Attridge. New York: Routledge, 1992.

―――. Edmund Husserl's *"Origins of Geometry": An Introduction*. Trans. John P. Leavey. Lincoln: U of Nebraska P, 1989.

―――. "Le Facteur de la vérité." *The Postcard: From Socrates to Freud and Beyond*. Trans. Alan Bass. Chicago: U of Chicago P, 1987. 413–96.

―――. "Inventions of the Other." *Reading de Man Reading*. Ed.

Lindsay Waters and Wlad Godzich. Minneapolis: U of Minnesota P, 1989. 54–74.

———. "JAC Interview." *(Inter)views: Cross-Disciplinary Perspectives on Rhetoric and Literacy*. Ed. Gary Olson and Irene Gale. Carbondale: Southern Illinois UP, 1991.

———. "La Loi du Genre/The Law of Genre." *Glyph* 7 (1981): 176–232.

———. *Margins of Philosophy*. Trans. Alan Bass. Chicago: U of Chicago P, 1982.

———. *Of Grammatology*. Trans. Gayatri Chakravorty Spivak. Baltimore: Johns Hopkins UP, 1976.

———. *Of Spirit: Heidegger and the Question*. Trans. Geoffrey Bennington and Rachel Bowlby. Chicago: U of Chicago P, 1989.

———. "Signature, Event, Context." Trans. Samuel Weber and Jeffrey Mehlman. *Limited Inc*. Evanston: Northwestern UP, 1988. 1–23.

———. "The Time of a Thesis." *Philosophy in France Today*. Ed. Alan Montefiore. Cambridge: Cambridge UP, 1983. 34–50.

———. "The White Mythology." *Margins of Philosophy*. Trans. Alan Bass. Chicago: U of Chicago P, 1982. 207–71.

Descartes, René. *Discourse on Method*. Trans. Elizabeth D. Haldane and G. R. T. Ross. Chicago: Encyclopedia Britannica, 1952. 41–68.

———. *Meditations on First Philosophy*. Trans. Elizabeth S. Haldane and G. R. T. Ross. Chicago: Encyclopedia Britannica, 1952. 69–103.

———. *Oeuvres*. Ed. Charles Adam and Paul Tannery. Paris: Ministère de l'instruction publique, 1945.

Elbow, Peter. *Embracing Contraries*. New York: Oxford UP, 1986.

Feyerabend, Paul. *Farewell to Reason*. London: Verso, 1987.

Fink, Bruce. "Alienation and Separation: Logical Moments of Lacan's Dialectic of Desire." *Newsletter of the Freudian Field* 4 (Spring/Fall 1990): 78–119.

Fish, Stanley. "Being Interdisciplinary Is So Very Hard to Do." *Profession 89*. New York: MLA, 1989. 15–22.

Frege, Gottleib. *Begriffshrift. From Frege to Godel: A Sourcebook in Mathematical Logic, 1879–1931*. Ed. and trans. Jean van Heijenoort. Cambridge, MA: Harvard UP, 1967. 147–78.

Furth, Montgomery. Translator's Introduction. *The Basic Laws of Mathematics*. By Gottleib Frege. Berkeley: U of California P, 1964. v–lix.

126

Gallop, Jane. *Reading Lacan*. Ithaca: Cornell UP, 1985.

Granon-Lafont, Jeanne. *La topologie ordinaire de Jacques Lacan*. Paris: Hors Point Ligne, 1987.

Grosz, Elizabeth. *Jacques Lacan: A Feminist Introduction*. London: Routledge, 1990.

Harding, Sandra. *Whose Science? Whose Knowledge?* Ithaca: Cornell UP, 1991.

Hardy, G. H. *Divergent Series*. Oxford: Clarendon, 1965.

Hintikka, Jaako. *Time and Necessity: Studies in Aristotle's Theory of Modality*. Oxford: Clarendon, 1973.

Hyde, Lewis. *The Gift: Imagination and the Erotic Life of Property*. New York: Vintage Books, 1983.

Jarratt, Susan. *Refiguring the Sophists*. Carbondale: Southern Illinois UP, 1989.

Johnson, Samuel. *Rasselas*. *Rasselas, Poems, and Selected Prose*. Ed. Betrand H. Bronson. New York: Holt, 1952.

Juranville, Alain. *Lacan et la philosophe*. Paris: Presses Universitaires de France, 1984.

Kant, Immanuel. "A Selection from *The Logic*: 'Of Concepts.' " *Universals and Particulars*. Ed. Sam Winters. New York: American Academic, 1992. 74–81.

Kennedy, George. *Classical Rhetoric and Its Christian and Secular Tradition from Ancient to Modern Times*. Chapel Hill: U of North Carolina P, 1980.

Kierkegaard, Søren. *The Concept of Irony*. Trans. Lee Capel. Bloomington: Indiana UP, 1968.

Kline, Morris. *Mathematical Thought from Ancient to Modern Times*. 3 vols. New York: Oxford UP, 1972.

———. *Mathematics for the Nonmathematician*. New York: Dover, 1967.

Koyré, Alexandre. *A Documentary History of the Problem of Fall from Kepler to Newton*. *Transactions of the American Philosophical Society* 45 (1932): 329–95.

Kristeva, Julia. "Psychoanalysis and the Polis." *The Kristeva Reader*. Ed. Toril Moi. New York: Columbia UP, 1986. 310–14.

Lacan, Jacques. "Agency of the Letter in the Unconscious" [L'instance de la lettre]. *Ecrits: A Selection*. Trans. Alan Sheridan. New York: Norton, 1980.

———. "Desire and the Interpretation of Desire in Hamlet." *Yale French Studies* 55 and 56 (1977): 41–62.

————. *Ecrits: A Selection*. Trans. Alan Sheridan. New York: Norton, 1980.

————. "Kant with Sade." Trans. James Swenson. *October* 51 (Winter 1989): 55–104.

————. "Logical Time and Anticipated Certainty." Trans. Bruce Fink. *Newsletter of the Freudian Field* 2 (Fall 1988): 4–22.

————. "The Meaning of the Phallus." *Ecrits: A Selection*. Trans. Alan Sheridan. New York: Norton, 1980. 281–91.

————. "Science and Truth." Trans. Bruce Fink. *Newsletter of the Freudian Field* 3 (Spring/Fall 1988): 4–29.

————. *Seminar II: The Ego in Freud's Theory and in the Technique of Psychoanalysis*. Trans. Sylvana Tomaselli. Notes by John Forrester. Ed. Jacques-Alain Miller. New York: Norton, 1988.

————. *Seminar VII: L'éthique de la psychanalyse*. Ed. Jacques-Alain Miller. Paris: Navarin, 1989.

————. *Seminar XI: The Four Fundamental Concepts of Psychoanalysis*. Ed. Jacques-Alain Miller. Trans. Alan Sheridan. New York: Norton, 1981.

————. *Seminar XX: Encore*. Ed. Jacques-Alain Miller. Paris: Seuil, 1975.

————. *Television*. Trans. Jeffrey Mehlman. Ed. Joan Copjec. New York: Norton, 1989.

Lachterman, David. *The Ethics of Geometry*. New York: Routledge, 1989.

Lakatos, Imre. *Mathematics, Science, and Epistemology*. Vol. 2 of *Philosophical Papers*. Cambridge: Cambridge, 1978.

Leavey, John. "Undecidables and Old Names." Preface. *Edmund Husserl's Origins of Geometry: An Introduction*. By Jacques Derrida. Trans. John Leavey. Lincoln: U of Nebraska P, 1989. 1–21.

Leibnitz, G. W. "Letter to the Mathematician Varignon [February 2, 1702]." *Leibnitz's Philosophical Papers and Letters*. Ed. and trans. Leroy Loemaker. Freiburg: Dordrecht, 1969.

————. *Opuscules et fragments inédits de Leibniz*. Ed. Louis Couturat. Hildescheim: G. Olms, 1961.

Merleau-Ponty, Maurice. "Phenomenology and the Sciences of Man." Trans. John Wild. *Phenomenology, Language and Sociology*. Ed. John O'Neill. London: Heinemann Educational Books, 1974. 227–79.

————. *Sense and Non-Sense*. Trans. Hubert L. Dreyfus. Evanston, IL: Northwestern UP, 1964.

———. *The Visible and the Invisible*. Ed. Claude Lefort. Trans. Alphonso Lingis. Evanston, IL: Northwestern UP, 1968.

Miller, Jacques-Alain. "The Analytic Experience." *Lacan and the Subject of Language*. Ed. Ellie Ragland-Sullivan with Mark Bracher. New York: Routledge, 1991, 83–99.

———. "Extimité." Unpublished course.

———. "A Reading of Some Details of Jacques Lacan's *Television*." *Newsletter of the Freudian Field* 4 (Spring/Fall 1990): 4–30.

———. "Suture (Elements of the Logic of the signifier)." *Screen* 18 (Winter 1977): 24–34.

———. "To Interpret the Cause." *Newsletter of the Freudian Field* 1 (Spring 1987): 23–46.

Miller, Judith. "Style Is the Man Himself." *Lacan and the Subject of Language*. Ed. Ellie Ragland-Sullivan with Mark Bracher. New York: Routledge, 1991. 111–20.

Pappus [of Alexandria]. *Collectio[nis] quae supersunt, e libris manu scriptis edidit latina interpretatione et commentariis instruxit Fredericus Hultsch*. Amsterdam: A. M. Hakkert, 1965.

Peano, Guiseppe. "From *Arithmeticas principia*." *Classics of Mathematics*. Ed. Ronald Calinger. Trans. Jean van Heijenoort. Oak Park, IL: Moore Publishing Co., 1982.

Popper, Karl. *The Logic of Scientific Discovery*. London: Hutchinson P, 1968.

Rabinovich, Diana. "Don Juan as Slave." *Newsletter of the Freudian Field*. 5 (Spring/Fall 1991): 86–95.

Ragland-Sullivan, Ellie. "Counting from 0 to 6: Lacan 'Suture,' and the Imaginary Order." *Lacan and Criticism*. Ed. Patrick Colm Hogan and Lalita Pandit. Athens: U of Georgia P, 1990. 31–63.

———. "Introduction to Lacan's Theory of Discourse Structure." Unpublished lecture. Spring 1990.

———. *Jacques Lacan and the Philosophy of Psychoanalysis*. Urbana: U of Illinois P, 1987.

———. "The Poetics of Lack." Unpublished lecture. Spring 1990.

Regnault, François. "Lacan and Experience." *Lacan and the Human Sciences*. Ed. Alexandre Leupin. Lincoln: U of Nebraska P, 1991. 43–58.

Rotman, Brian. *Signifying Nothing: The Semiotics of Zero*. New York: St. Martin's, 1987.

Roudinesco, Elisabeth. *Jacques Lacan and Co*. Trans. Jeffrey Mehlman. Chicago: U of Chicago P, 1990.

Rucker, Rudy. *The Science and Philosophy of the Infinite*. New York: Bantam, 1982.

Samuels, Robert. "Logical Time and Jouissance." *Newsletter of the Freudian Field* 4 (Spring/Fall 1990): 69–77.

Sartre, Jean-Paul. "Why Write?" *Critical Theory since Plato*. Ed. Hazard Adams. New York: Harcourt, 1971. 1059–68.

Schleifer, Ronald. *Rhetoric and Death*. Urbana: University of Illinois Press, 1990.

Smith, Kathy. "Making Much of Time." Diss., Missouri, 1989.

Thom, René. *Mathematical Models of Morphogenesis*. Trans. W. M. Brookes and D. Rand. New York: John Wiley, 1983.

Toulmin, Stephen. *The Uses of Argument*. Cambridge: Cambridge UP, 1958.

Ulmer, Gregory. *Applied Grammatology*. Baltimore: Johns Hopkins UP, 1985.

———. "Handbook for a Theory Hobby" *Visible Language*. 8 (Spring 1988): 399–422.

———. *Teletheory: Grammatology in the Age of Video*. New York: Routledge, 1989.

Wilden, Anthony. "Lacan and the Discourse of the Other." *Speech and Language in Psychoanalysis*. Trans. and ed. Anthony Wilden. Baltimore: Johns Hopkins UP, 1985.

Wittgenstein, Ludwig. *The Blue and Brown Books*. New York: Harper, 1958.

———. *Tractatus Logico-Philosophicus*. Trans. C. K. Ogden. London: Routledge and Kegan Paul, 1922.

Žižek, Slavoj. *For They Know Not What They Do*. London: Verso, 1991.

———. *The Sublime Object of Ideology*. London: Verso, 1989.

INDEX

Academic knowledge, 86. *See also* Discourse

Acconci, Vito, 114n.19

Alienation: Lacan's treatment of, 55–56, 59; relation to metaphor/metonymy, 69

Aristotle, xv, 24; audience, 92; body, definition of, 47; chance as cause, 113n.13; *dunamis,* treatment of, 26, 30–31, 33–34; god as prime mover, 48–49; habit of mind, definition of, 32–33; knowledge, definition of, 44; *Metaphysics,* 23, 27, 29, 32–33; *Nichomachean Ethics,* xii; the now and, 37–39, 81; *The Prior Analytics,* 106; relationality, treatment of, 3; *Rhetoric,* 27–28, 48, 92; rhetoric, definition of, 29–31; signs, treatment of, 106–7, 122n.19; *techne,* 33, 34; truth, on the discovery of, 39; void, treatment of, 117n.5

Attridge, Derek, 115n.20

Baumlin, James, 35, 116n.5

Benvenuto, Bice, 66

Bifurcation, 56, 111n.1

Bizzell, Patricia, xii

Body: metonymy and, 56; proof and, 41

Carpe Diem poetry, 37, 117n.7

Causality: Lacan's treatment of, 60

Choice, 56

Citizen Kane [character], 58

Cocteau, Jean, 60–61

Cogito. See Descartes, René

Covino, William, 31–32, 116n.1

Deconstruction, 18, 98

Deliberative speech: time and, 43

Derrida, Jacques, xv, 1–2, 18, 111n.2; *Acts of Literature,* 115n.20; being, treatment of, 64; common readings of, 12; *Edmund Husserl's "Origins of Geometry": An Introduction,* 98; the elliptical and, 14; "Le Facteur de la vérité," 98; genealogical philosophy and, 2, 13–19; genre, treatment of, xi; grafting as method, 11; identity, treatment of, 64; imperatives, treatment of, 20; infinity, treatment of, 73; invagination and double invagination in, 14, 17, 19; "The Law of Genre," 13–14; *Margins of Philosophy,* 13, 14, 114n.17; metonymy in work of, 3; *Of Grammatology,* 11, 122n.14; *Of Spirit: Heidegger and the Question,* 20; reflective knowledge and, 14; rhetoric, his dismissal of, 14; set theory and, 14, 16; "Signature, Event, Context," 98; supplementary in, 18; "The White Mythology," 13

Descartes, René, 1–2, 8–10; *cogito,* xi, 5–8; God, assertion of, 7–8; infinity, treatment of, 73; innate knowledge and, 16; metaphor in

131

DAVID METZGER is an assistant professor of English at Old Dominion University, where he teaches writing. He is the editor of the Lacan journal *Bien Dire* and has published essays on medieval and Renaissance rhetorical theory, ancient nonclassical rhetorics, and myth. He has edited a forthcoming issue of *Pre/Text* called "Lacan and the Question of Writing" and a forthcoming collection of essays, with Gwendolyn Morgan, entitled "Reading and Writing in the New Middle Ages." Metzger is currently writing a textbook with Lynda Sexson on the Bible as literature and finishing a book on ancient Egyptian rhetoric.